SECOND EMPIRE AND COMMUNE

Second Empire and Commune: France 1848–1871

SECOND EDITION

WILLIAM H.C. SMITH

LONGMAN
LONDON AND NEW YORK

Pearson Education Limited
Edinburgh Gate,
Harlow, Essex CM20 2JE, United Kingdom
and Associated Companies throughout the world.

Visit us on the World Wide Web at:
http://www.pearsoneduc.com

First published 1985
Second edition 1996

ISBN 0 582 28705 7 PPR

British Library Cataloguing in Publication Data

A catalogue record for this book is available from
the British Library

Library of Congress Cataloging-in-Publication Data

Smith, W. H. C. (William Herbert Cecil), 1925-
    Second Empire and Commune : France, 1848-1871 / W.H.C. Smith. --
2nd ed.
        p. cm. -- (Seminar studies in history)
    Includes bibliographical references and index.
    ISBN 0-582-28705-7
    1. France--History--1848-1870. 2. Franco-Prussian War,
1870-1871. 3. Paris (France)--History--Commune, 1871. I. Title.
II. Series.
DC276.S64 1996
944.07--dc20   95-43293
                                                                      CIP

    7 6 5 4 3 2
    06 05 04 03 02

Set by 7 in 10/12 Sabon Roman
Printed in Malaysia, GPS_

CONTENTS

EDITORIAL FOREWORD

Such is the pace of historical enquiry in the modern world that there is an ever-widening gap between the specialist article or monograph, incorporating the results of current research, and general surveys, which inevitably become out of date. *Seminar Studies in History* are designed to bridge this gap. The books are written by experts in their field who are not only familiar with the latest research but have often contributed to it. They are frequently revised, in order to take account of new information and interpretations. They provide a selection of documents to illustrate major themes and provoke discussion, and also a guide to further reading. Their aim is to clarify complex issues without over-simplifying them, and to stimulate readers into deepening their knowledge and understanding of major themes and topics.

ROGER LOCKYER

NOTE ON REFERENCING SYSTEM

Readers should note that numbers in square brackets [5] refer them to the corresponding entry in the Bibliography at the end of the book (specific page numbers are given in italics). A number in square brackets preceded by *Doc.* [*Doc. 5*] refers readers to the corresponding item in the Documents section which follows the main text.

ACKNOWLEDGEMENTS

The publishers would like to thank Princeton University Press for permission to reproduce a table from Cameron, E. Rondon, *France and the Economic Development of Europe*, p. 88. Copyright © 1961 by Princeton University Press.

FOREWORD

Peter Jones's book *The 1848 Revolutions*, published in the same series and now in its second edition, provides an excellent description and analysis of the events which form a prelude to my own work, and I have therefore given only a cursory account of those events in France. For further information I refer the reader to Peter Jones's Seminar Study.

I should like to make plain that unless otherwise indicated, all translations which occur in this book are my own.

PART ONE: THE BACKGROUND

1 THE 1848 REVOLUTION AND ITS CONSEQUENCES

The Revolution of February 1848 in Paris which toppled the government of Louis-Philippe was as much of a shock to its 'organisers' as it was to those whom it overthrew. The conservative dynastic opposition who had attacked the policies of the King and Guizot in the Assembly had wanted reform, not revolution. Even the more radical elements who had combined public eating with political speeches in the 'Banquet Campaign' of 1846–48 had wanted electoral reform, not a rejection of the regime. It was the failure of both government and opposition to see the basic weakness of the Guizot system which produced the unforeseen events. None of the conservative reformist groups could control the situation they had unwittingly brought about, particularly in Paris, while the King himself, old and dispirited, proved useless as a sheet anchor in the storm [28].

All that could be done was to try and find a quick solution which might (with luck) satisfy the aspirations of those who clamoured for political reform by proclaiming a Republic and instituting universal male suffrage. As for the partisans of social reform, they were to be bought off by the government's declaring the right to work and by the institution of National Workshops to provide employment for those who had none. An amalgam of political figures, ranging from former ministers of the fallen regime to socialist-minded Republicans, managed to cobble together a programme which it was hoped would pacify the more turbulent elements in society while buying time in which to restore order. But the political spectrum covered by the members of the government, and the conflicting ideas which they represented, could not provide a durable or stable system, and within a few months of its existence the basic differences began to show. Increasing rural disorder, coupled with unrest in the major cities, led inevitably to a polarisation of views in which the conservative elements, led by Thiers and Odilon Barrot (former Orleanists), began to push for a restoration of law and order. Encouraged by the election of a conservative Constituent Assembly, they began to work towards this end, but inevitably, the more the Right seemed to be triumphant, the more the radical elements became disenchanted, and in May an insurrection occurred in Paris during which the mob invaded the Chamber of Deputies. So alarmed were the conservative elements by this event that, when a second insurrection broke out in June, the government ordered its suppression by military force [29]. The immediate effects of this suppression were to alienate the Parisian workers and to antagonise all the progressive elements in the country. At the same time, the repercussions of the 'June Days' produced the one thing which virtually all groups in the Assembly feared – namely a rise in the popularity of Louis Napoleon Bonaparte.

THE EMERGENCE OF LOUIS NAPOLEON

The son of Louis Bonaparte and Hortense de Beauharnais, daughter of the Empress Josephine, Louis Napoleon was the only member of the Imperial family who had shown a determination to maintain the cause of Bonapartism. To him it was not simply an historical curiosity, but an ongoing political doctrine to whose furtherance he resolved to dedicate himself. In 1836 he attempted to lead a revolt by the military garrison at Strasbourg, and although this ended in failure it proved to be a triumph for his public image, in that people were made aware of the existence of a Bonaparte who was prepared to do more than live on the glory of his name. To maintain this interest he resolved to put forward his political views in print. In 1839 he published his 'Napoleonic Ideas', setting out his interpretation of his uncle's life and work and also outlining in some detail his own plans for a possible future regime based on these Napoleonic ideas. The book was a success, selling over 500,000 copies in a few years and being translated into all the major European languages.

Encouraged by the book's success and by this apparent upsurge of interest in Bonapartism as a political creed, the Prince decided on a second attempt to seize power. In 1840 he left England, where he had been living in exile, and with a small group of followers set out across the Channel to Boulogne. Once more the attempt to rouse the garrison in his favour was a failure, but it seems that, although unsuccessful, the plot had fairly wide ramifications. The government was in any event sufficiently alarmed by the affair to try Louis Napoleon and to sentence him to perpetual imprisonment in the fortress of Ham in northern France. But 'perpetual' in this case had been reduced by his successful escape to a mere six years and the outbreak of the February Revolution in Paris found him living in London. Imprisonment had not weakened his resolve; it had in fact strengthened it. All that had happened was that he was convinced that the road to power lay through the ballot box and that the introduction of universal male suffrage had made his victory virtually inevitable. He believed this because he was convinced that the attitudes of the ruling elites did not represent the wishes of the mass of the people, who had remained loyal to the memory of Napoleon, and whose latent Bonapartism needed only to be given a means of expression for this to be proved. Events bore out the correctness of Louis' political analysis.

The hostility of the governmental groups towards him was shown as early as 28 February, when virtually as soon as he arrived in Paris he was requested to leave. This he did, but his agents remained behind and in June they saw to it that the Prince's name was put forward for the by-elections which were being held. He was elected for all four seats, including one in Paris, but he refused to sit in the Assembly which still remained overtly hostile. Indeed the government authorised his arrest should he return to France.

As already indicated, the June insurrection in Paris sharply polarised the political situation by frightening the conservatives and the men of order, who now felt that the whole fabric of society was likely to be overthrown unless means could be found to prevent it. In the short run, General Cavaignac had suppressed the rising, with considerable brutality, but action such as this could only provide a temporary and not a long-term solution to the political problem. It was with this knowledge that Louis Napoleon put forward his candidature for the by-elections in September. Once again he was elected to all those seats for which he had stood, including a seat in Paris where he easily came top of the poll. This time the Assembly yielded and in September the Prince arrived in Paris. Then he set himself quietly and unostentatiously to fill the role of deputy while preparing for higher things. Convinced of his popularity, as revealed by his electoral successes, he had resolved to stand for the Presidential elections in December. His confidence was not misplaced for he was elected with four million more votes than his nearest rival, Cavaignac. Those hostile to Louis Napoleon have interpreted his election as the 'triumph of reaction', but it would be truer to say that reaction had triumphed during the 'June Days'.

Therefore, to see the election of Louis Napoleon as a simple continuation of this process is to misunderstand both the nature of Bonapartism and the political situation as it had developed within France since February. As a result of the shifts in the political equilibrium during this period, Bonapartism, from having been simply one factor in French political thinking, had emerged as the answer to the problems which 1848 had posed. To the conservative elements Louis Napoleon represented order and strong government, with the additional advantage that his previous career had not involved him with the existing political elites. Men like Thiers, Molé, and Barrot, for whom 1848 had been a disaster, could hope to use and control the new President [29; 43]. To the workers Louis Napoleon did not simply represent a return to a previous condition, that is to say, to the First Empire, but promised a new policy which would take account of their grievances. In his propagandist writings, such as the *Suppression of Poverty* (1844), Louis Napoleon had manifested both interest in, and sympathy with, the problems of the working people and had always insisted upon the necessity for the introduction of universal suffrage [41; 43]. Furthermore, he was clearly untainted by the repression of the 'June Days', since at the time he had not even been a member of the Assembly which had authorised General Cavaignac to suppress the insurrection.

THE IMPACT OF UNIVERSAL SUFFRAGE

As for the masses of rural voters, the power of the name which Louis Napoleon bore combined with their desire to go against the wishes of the authorities who were, for the most part, hostile to the Presidential candidature of the Prince. In addition, the peasants bitterly resented the 45 centimes' tax imposed by the Republican government in March 1848 in an attempt to cover the budgetary deficit. Since this was associated with the Republican regime and its representatives, it provided them with a specific reason for their rejection of the new system. The voting for the Constituent Assembly had already shown how far this rejection went; the opportunity to reinforce it came with the chance to vote for Louis Napoleon, particularly as those who had been elected in March made no attempt to deal with rural problems and the peasantry felt that there was nothing to be hoped for from the Assembly. That was why, in December, they categorically refused to consider any other candidature but that of Louis Napoleon. In the Bordeaux region the Procurator General, representing the authority of the government, attempted to stem the rising tide of support for Louis

Napoleon, only to be told by peasant spokesmen that: 'We listened to you once and we have nothing to congratulate ourselves about in having done so; this time we want to go our own way.' Other government officials reported the same attitude to be prevalent in widely separated regions of France. Odilon Barrot, one of the leading Orleanist members of the ruling elite, wrote to a friend on 9 December that: 'The country people, the real political force, are in no doubt: everywhere on my journeys I've been met with cries of "Vive Napoléon". These cries express different discontents, some of which are dangerous because they show the desire of a part of the people to defy the well-to-do whom they suppose to be favourable to another candidate (Cavaignac)' [29; 44].

It may also be that the peasantry were taking their revenge for thirty years of exclusion from the political machinery which, since 1815, had been in the hands of small, elite groups who had made and unmade regimes and governments. These activities had usually been carried out 'in the name of the French people' but the people themselves had for the most part been non-participants in the process. The granting of universal suffrage meant that this type of exclusion was no longer possible, and the results were to mark a decisive change in the whole nature and structure of the French political system [73].

The immediate effect of what Marx called 'the peasant insurrection' was to make Louis Napoleon President of the Republic with five and a half million votes as against his nearest rival, Cavaignac, who polled just under a million and a half. As one contemporary commentator said (with slight exaggeration): 'Louis Napoleon has six million more good reasons [for ruling] than Louis-Philippe'. The question now was: would the man who had said 'I shall always govern in the interests of the masses' be able to fulfil his ambition? Three things would determine the answer: one was the nature of the Constitution; the second was the behaviour of the political elite; the third, and perhaps the most important, was the ability of Louis Napoleon to deal with both.

THE FAILURE OF THE 1848 CONSTITUTION

The committee which drew up the constitution of the Republic sought to avoid those things which, it seemed to them, had weakened previous regimes; that is, an executive which was too strong and a representative body which was too weak. The solution which they offered was the creation of a strong executive tempered by the control of an Assembly – both to be elected by universal suffrage. The President was given extensive powers of legislation, but all his acts had to be countersigned by the ministers responsible for the various branches of government. However, since the head of state was also the head of the government, the constitution had, in fact, created a double responsibility while at the same time making it quite unclear as to who should have the ultimate power in the event of a clash of wills. Since both parties, that is the President and the Assembly, could claim a mandate from the people, both had, in democratic terms, equal authority – with one significant difference. The Assembly, with its 750 deputies, represented the multiplicity of the voters, whereas the President, one person, represented the singularity of their choice. Odilon Barrot pointed this out in a letter to a friend in 1848: 'Now, under the name of "constitution" we have set up a fight to the death between a president and a single chamber, a fight which confronts the country with the inevitable alternative of despotism or anarchy. God knows what will become of this constitution. I feel sorry for the unfortunate President with his vast attributions and his immense powerlessness.' The constitution precluded any easy solution to the problems which its working might cause by prohibiting any attempt at revising its clauses until three years had elapsed. Even then, any motion requiring change would have to be voted in three successive sittings by a three-fourths' majority of those voting. It has been said that this was a wise measure, adopted in imitation of the constitution of the United States of America, but in the American scheme there was room for amendments which the French 'copy' did not provide.

Everything it contained seemed, therefore, designed to make the constitution dangerously unworkable; the behaviour of the political groups hastened the breakdown [22; 43].

PART TWO: DESCRIPTIVE ANALYSIS

2   REPUBLIC AND EMPIRE

The conservative groups which had fused together as 'The Party of Order' were the victims of their own political ambivalence. They had hoped to create a Republic which would be conservative and stable and which they could control by their own efforts, but the successive shocks caused by the insurrections of May and June 1848 had led them to doubt their ability to maintain control. For that reason they had been forced to accept the logic of the Presidential election of December, since it seemed that only Louis Napoleon was capable of providing a unifying force and a rallying point for the country as a whole. In the hope that they had a Prince Consort rather than a Prince President, the Party of Order, led by Thiers, Molé, and Barrot, immediately tried to surround the President with men of their own persuasion. Hence the first ministry became known as the 'Ministry of the Captivity' with Odilon Barrot in the role of chief warder. Louis Napoleon had no confidence in the ministry, and neither had the Assembly, but there was as yet no profit for anybody to be found in pressing for changes. It must be remembered that the new President was like a tourist in a foreign country; his longest sojourn in France had been the six years spent in captivity in the fortress at Ham, to which he had been condemned after his attempted *coup d'état* in 1840 at Boulogne. As one of his partisans, Persigny, remarked: 'The Prince did not know one man of importance who could serve him and had not a friend whom he could suitably make minister'. So the Party of Order felt reasonably hopeful that it could force the President along the path it wanted him to take, and he at first seemed docile, hastily retreating from any possibility of a clash between himself and the ministry.

Events, however, conspired to break this period of calm. The elections of May 1849 revealed a greater degree of polarisation in the country than had existed in 1848. On the one hand the 'Liberal Union', as the Party of Order styled itself, won 450 out of the 750 seats, while the radical 'Democ-Soc' Republicans won 210, the moderate Republicans obtaining about 60. But the results were not comforting for the conservatives if one counted the actual number of votes cast: 3,268,000 for the candidates of the Liberal Union, 2,368,000 for the Republicans. At this rate it seemed likely that the next election in 1852 could well give the Radicals a majority in the Assembly.

The Party of Order panicked, particularly because in June 1849 there was an insurrection in Paris led by Ledru-Rollin, one of the radical Republican leaders of '48'. It was easily suppressed, but it further alarmed the conservatives. In their desperation they were forced closer to Louis Napoleon who, taking advantage of the situation, set up a new ministry in October 1849 composed of men who were nearer to him in sentiment. As a second desperate measure and in an attempt to exclude the poorer sections of the country, the conservatives forced a law through the Assembly in May 1850 which reduced the number of voters by nearly 3,000,000. They had thus destroyed one of the basic premises of the Republic and arbitrarily altered the constitution. At this point the President decided to begin his own bid for power.

Louis Napoleon may have been a stranger to French political life; he was no novice when it came to political calculation. He saw quite clearly how the actions of the Party of Order could only weaken their position in the country, which interpreted their manoeuvrings as an attack on the whole democratic structure in the interests of the Notables. In the circumstances this could only increase his popularity, which he now deliberately cultivated by embarking on a series of tours of France. In his public speeches he lost no opportunity to stress how his desire to carry through a social and economic programme, in the interest of *all* classes of society, was being frustrated by the selfish and unprogressive attitude of the majority in the Assembly [*Doc. 1*]. He also indicated that the only way out of the impasse was to bring about a revision of the constitution which would enable him to stand for a second term of office. The constitution made the outgoing President ineligible for re-election, but the electoral reform of 1850 had already made a nonsense of this clause, whether or not that had been its intention. According to the constitution the President needed one-fifth of the votes cast to be elected. By altering the number of voters it now meant that, proportionally, the successful candidate would have to poll *one-third* of the votes. If he did not receive this number then the Assembly had, constitutionally, the right to elect the President – who could be of their choosing. There is strong evidence to suggest that, should this situation arise, the Party of Order envisaged the nomination of one of the sons of Louis-Philippe, thus restoring the monarchy and reverting more or less to the system of 1830–48 [6; 44].

The refusal of the Assembly to restore universal suffrage in full and to revise the constitution in accordance with Louis Napoleon's request led to a complete breakdown of the political dialogue between the two. An attempt, in November 1851, by the Assembly to remove control of the armed forces from the President revealed that a final showdown could not be long delayed [*Doc. 2*].

Louis Napoleon was, after many hesitations, ready to face this prospect. The evidence of his popularity throughout the country at large was incontrovertible; he had now placed his own supporters in the key ministries, and he had carefully prepared his plans for a *coup d'état*. Furthermore, it was clear that continuing political instability was having serious effects on the economy. Trade was languishing, investment was virtually at a standstill and fear of the future brought about a climate of increasing despair, not helped by serious outbreaks of cholera which further unsettled and frightened all classes of society.

It seems certain that an important factor in Louis Napoleon's calculations as to his future actions lay in the attitude of the Republicans in the Assembly. Many of them, confronted with the reactionary obstructionism of the Conservatives, seemed willing to support him – not least because of a suspicion that the Party of Order wanted to gain control of the army with the aim of carrying through a *coup* in their own interests. This would probably bring about a restoration of the monarchy – a prospect the Republicans regarded with loathing. A majority of them, therefore, voted against the attempt to take away the President's control of the armed forces, and many of their leaders, in their speeches, indicated their support for his position. But in the last resort the Republicans would not follow through their attitudes and take up the cry for constitutional revision. By so doing they made the *coup d'état* inevitable. It is probable that Louis Napoleon would have preferred a prolongation of his powers, but in the long run he would not draw back from a confrontation. He had sought power, had achieved it, and the whole force of his personality and character, with its strong streak of fatalism, precluded any abandoning of what he considered to be his destiny. In a conscious echo of Julius Caesar's famous action, he named the *coup d'état* 'Operation Rubicon'.

LOUIS NAPOLEON'S *COUP D'ÉTAT* – 2 DECEMBER 1851

So carefully organised was the *coup* that in its initial stages it went through smoothly. The swift arrest of leading political figures and the rounding up of suspects both in Paris and in the provinces meant that any resistance was left without coherent leadership or organised direction. The Comte de Falloux, a Royalist, who had been a minister in 1848–9, described in his *Memoires* how surprise was the key element in the plan:

> M. Thiers was seized in his bed and was as shocked as he had been on 24 February (1848). General Le Flô, at the Palais Bourbon (seat of the National Assembly), found his bedroom invaded by a former comrade-in-arms, Colonel Espinasse, to whom, it appears, he had recently shown the secret staircase by which it was possible to reach the sentries on duty and thus to get to the Invalides where a regiment was quartered. General Changarnier and General de la Moricière were so cleverly and so suddenly seized while they were sleeping that they had not even time to grab hold of the pistols which they kept beside them. Only General Bedeau was able to get into the street where he raised an outcry against the attempt to arrest him. He was forcibly put into a cab which was waiting near his house and driven off. It was the same story everywhere. ... Few members of the Left offered any serious resistance. Only Baudin, a deputy who represented 'The Mountain' (the radical left), found the death which he sought on a barricade and which he accepted with real heroism (3 *p. 309*].

Baudin had in fact been killed on 3 December while trying to persuade the workers in the Saint Antoine district of Paris to oppose the *coup*. He had no success, the workers showing themselves to be either indifferent or hostile, but his death was to be of significance when the Empire came under hostile attacks in the late 1860s. The days of 3 and 4 December did see sporadic resistance spring up in Paris and there were casualties, particularly on the 4th, when a panic fusillade by soldiers resulted in some sixty deaths and a large number of wounded.

However, the most significant event of the whole affair was not the shooting down of demonstrators on the night of 4 December in Paris, but the outbreak of revolts in the provinces. For the first time in the history of French revolutions, the provinces were more insurrectionary than the capital. It was as a result of the outbreaks in the provinces that the largest number of arrests was made. The figures are disputed, but it seems certain that nearly 27,000 people were brought before the special courts set up to judge those who had been involved in the resistance. There were few death sentences, but thousands were sent to penal settlements or to forced exile in Algeria, while others were exiled elsewhere. It must be remembered that it was not just those who were arrested who suffered, but also their families and their friends. Many of the 5,000 who were released within days of their arrest found that the stigma attached to their name led to unemployment, financial ruin, and the destruction of their families.

The repression was therefore brutal, yet it can be argued that it would have been far worse had not some restraints been exercised on those who were carrying it out. Significantly, one of the most restraining influences was that of Louis Napoleon himself [36]. However, it would be wrong to underestimate either the nature of the repression or its effects. The conservative classes' fear of 'the Reds' and their hatred of them had been building up over a period of three years, and their position in the administration and the judiciary enabled them now to give full vent 'legally' to the suppression of those whom they loathed and feared. If Louis Napoleon had hoped to break free of the control of the conservatives by making his *coup d'état*, he soon found the error of his ways. He had in fact delivered himself up to them, for the Republicans' hatred of the *coup* of 2 December meant that their opposition to his regime was implacable, and there was thus no political counterpoise available [*Doc. 3*]. It was this lack of a political alternative which led to many of the problems of the regime from 1851 to 1870, and, as old sins cast long shadows, was to condition the nature of the Third Republic.

THE CHARACTER OF THE NEW REGIME

The development of the governmental system following the *coup d'état*, falls into two stages: the Decennial Republic, which lasted from January 1852 until December 1852, followed by the Second Empire which lasted until September 1870.

In the proclamation which accompanied the *coup d'état*, Louis Napoleon restored universal suffrage in its entirety and set out the bases of his political programme, promising that the whole project would be submitted to a plebiscite [*Doc. 4*]. The results of the plebiscite, which were in no way rigged, were startling. Over seven million voted their approval of the project, and by implication of the *coup* itself, while the 'No' votes were a mere six hundred thousand.

Louis Napoleon considered himself 'absolved' of his illegal *coup* by this vote, though all observers agreed that he never overcame his unhappiness at the necessity for it.

In January 1852, under the direction of Louis Napoleon, a new constitution was drawn up. The President of the Republic, elected for ten years, was the key to the whole structure: '. . . [he] is responsible to the French people to whom he has always the right to appeal'. The Bonapartist idea of authoritarian democracy, 'confidence from below, authority from above', thus found its definition, just as it had under Napoleon I. This creation of a strong and responsible executive entailed, of necessity, a diminution in the power of the Legislative Body. Therefore the ministers were appointed by the President, and responsible to him, while the Senate, guardian of the constitution, was composed of Presidential nominees. The Legislative Body was directed in its role of law-maker by the Council of State which was charged with the preparation of the actual laws themselves. Severe press laws restricted the reporting of political speeches and debates, including those of the Legislature, since its business was to discuss, not debate, the projects submitted to it. A fundamental tenet of Bonapartism was that political parties were factious and divisive and that nothing which might encourage them should be permitted [37]. Hence the members of the Legislature found themselves deprived of a press which would enable them to 'play politics'.

However, the constitution, although rigid in appearance, did permit the possibility of change, but any fundamental alteration would have to be submitted to the people for ratification – which is what happened in 1870.

Given that Louis Napoleon was heir to the Bonapartist legacy of the great Emperor, and given the highly personal nature of the Presidential constitution, the future development of the regime could hardly be in doubt. It was therefore with an air of inevitability that on 2 December 1852 the Empire was proclaimed, Louis Napoleon becoming Emperor of the French as Napoleon III. A further plebiscite was held to ratify this change. Nearly eight million voted 'Yes', some two hundred and fifty thousand voted No', though significantly, two million gave no answer at all. In his first meeting with the Senators and Legislators in his new role the Emperor adjured them to 'Help me, gentlemen, to found a stable government which has for its basis religion, honest dealing, justice, and the love of the suffering classes' [10].

To describe the Second Empire as a dictatorship is to miss the point. The government was authoritarian, but at no time, except for the immediate aftermath of December 1852, was France without representative institutions or a code of law. Napoleon III saw his task as quite simple; to heal the divisions in French society, to promote economic and social well-being, and to recover for France her position in Europe. To achieve these ends he was convinced that there must be firm, efficient and orderly government which would end the convulsions of the last thirty-odd years.

Politically he sought reconciliation, and to this end the constitution did not prohibit opposition, provided it came within the legal framework, i.e. within the Legislative Body. It is true that at elections the government ran 'official candidates', who enjoyed the support and overt backing of the local authorities, but this was not a new practice, nor did it preclude the activities of non-official candidates. In the election of 1852 three Republicans were elected, but since they refused to take the oath of loyalty to the constitution they were disbarred. In 1857 five Republicans were elected and, having taken the oath, sat in the Chamber, where they constituted a critical opposition presence. 'The Five', as they were called, were a mere handful among the 261 members, but they were more than a token group, and in the 1863 elections their number rose to fifteen.

OPPOSITION MOVEMENTS

It should not be imagined, however, that this tiny 'official' opposition represented the sum of those hostile to many aspects of the regime's policies. Hostility came in various guises and most of those who were elected as deputies represented the same conservative groupings who accepted the Empire with a 'yes – but' attitude. The Legislative Body, although restricted in its activities, was far from docile, and since the constitution gave it control of the budget it could, and did, make its opposition felt. It must be remembered that in the constitutional development of the Empire the Legislature exercised pressure as well as the Executive. The first loosening up of the tight controls, which came in 1860–61, bears this out, since while it is true that these modifications represented the will of the Emperor, the form which they took was tailored to meet specific demands of the Legislative Body. Napoleon III was anxious to carry out his reforms because he sincerely believed in a progressive liberalisation of the regime, but the difficulties arising from working with a frequently recalcitrant Chamber expedited the process. The key area of disagreement was that of finance, and one Republican deputy estimated that: 'It was the budgetary commissions (of the Chamber) which after 1852 began the work of reconstituting the constitutional regime'. Even a cursory reading of the proceedings of the Chamber shows that this was so [20; 44].

Added to this financial leverage was the fact that, according to the constitution, ministers were not permitted to appear in the Chamber. This situation was increasingly found to be unsatisfactory since if, on the one hand, they could not be attacked and questioned about policy, on the other, they could not defend or explain it.

So by the 1860–61 reforms the Chamber gained the right to discuss the Address from the Throne, to have their discussions published in the newspapers, and, as a first step towards ministerial responsibility, to have in their midst ministers (albeit without portfolio) who could be questioned and made to discuss policy. Perhaps the most important change came in November 1861, when the Emperor abandoned his constitutional right to authorise supplementary or extraordinary budgetary credits when the Legislative Body was not in session. Henceforward the deputies would have continuous and complete financial control.

The notable feature of this constitutional development is that it was being accomplished peacefully. True, there was opposition, but it was legal, and since the regime had not envisaged unanimity of opinion, but rather diversity within a framework of unity, it could be said to be achieving its aim. Napoleon III's expressed desire to unite French society appeared to be in a way realising itself in spite of the unrelenting hostility of sections of the political class. The *coup d'état* had led to the arrest and proscription of many among the educated and professional members of society, people who were well able to wage a literary and political campaign against the regime. They lost no opportunity to do so, operating within the shelter of institutions such as the prestigious French Academy. During the entire period from 1851 to 1870 the Academy chose to elect to its ranks those who were known to be opponents of the Empire. In this way it was possible publicly to manifest both hostility to, and contempt for, Napoleon III without running the risk of disagreeable consequences. The mere fact of being an Academician was a protection in itself.

It was not simply the political policies of the Emperor which caused a high level of discontent; his social and economic policies provoked even greater resentment among the conservative groups. Given that these groups had not lost anything of their fear and dislike of what Thiers called 'the vile multitude', it was inevitable that social reforms destined to improve the living and working conditions of the latter should meet with hostility. This opposition was not confined to sulking or grumbling; at all levels of the judiciary and the administration the entrenched authority of the conservatives could be used to slow down or thwart the Emperor's schemes. Those who dismiss Napoleon III as a 'despot', acting at will, have failed to consider the strength of his opponents. Even at the level of the Council of State, appointed by the Emperor, and in theory subordinate to his executive authority, ways were found of blocking his social programme. No wonder Napoleon III complained: 'I would have done much more for the working population than I did if I had found firm support in the Council of State' [50][*Doc. 5*].

As a consequence, many of the actions carried out from 1852 might seem no better than acts of paternal charity, designed rather to buy off than to satisfy the needs of the workers [62]. Yet much was achieved: the construction of reasonable dwellings to be let at economical rents; help and encouragement to cooperative societies; a state-subsidised organisation to assist the needy in times of sickness or to help with the expenses of a death; the opening of two convalescent homes for workers who were injured in the course of their employment; and, at the end of the reign, a plan for an old-age pension scheme, which came to nothing because the Empire fell. All of this may be dismissed as 'bribery', but those who were recipients of the funds which were distributed, or were sheltered in times of sickness, may have felt less critical. They may even have been glad to exchange an existence at virtual subsistence level for one of relative ease [34].

The most important achievement of the Emperor in his fight to help the workers was, however, the legalisation of trade unions and the granting of the right to strike.

Faced with opposition from the conservative groups to any change in the legal status of trade unions, Napoleon III forced the issue by pardoning those workers who were sentenced for infringing the laws which forbade organisation and strikes. In 1862 the Emperor's action in quashing the sentences of a group of printing workers, and the discussion it provoked, led finally to an acceptance of the inevitable. If the law was to be made virtually useless, then it had better go. And so, in 1864, amid much grumbling from the employers and the conservative groups in general, the laws were repealed and the right to strike conceded. In 1868 the employers received another blow with the repeal of a further article of the Civil Code by which, in the event of a dispute about payment for labour, the employers' word was always taken in the matter of setting a wage [13; 58] [*Doc.6*].

ECONOMIC DEVELOPMENTS

The general background to this 'state socialism' was the period of great economic growth and an accompanying general prosperity which marked the whole of the period from 1852 to 1870, and which continued, in fact, until the early 1880s.

The political stability which the regime provided was favourable to the increase of investment, and this, combined with the official policy of encouraging major public works, led to a spectacular change in the economic structure of France. While it is true that there were periods of fluctuation in growth, and even more true that not all sections of society benefited equally from the economic boom, there is no doubt that overall there was a rise in the standard of living. For the workers, the early part of the reign was marked by an increase in wages, which kept pace with the rise in prices, though it appears that in the 1860s there was a widening disparity between wages and prices. This factor, combined with the workers' developing sense of their power, led to a series of strikes in 1869–70 which seemed to indicate that Napoleon III had failed in his attempt to reconcile masses and classes, though it is possible to interpret the movement in various ways.

Undoubtedly the class which benefited most from the industrial and economic growth was the class with money to invest or with access to borrowing in order to invest. Opportunities for promoting all sorts of schemes presented themselves and the period was marked by scandals which resulted from a too great showing of 'the unacceptable face of capitalism'. To judge the achievements of the regime by concentrating on the scandals which marred it, however, is not particularly constructive, and the Second Empire did not establish a monopoly on shady deals. It should also perhaps be recorded that the government attempted to control wild speculation and that Napoleon III on several occasions publicly condemned it. But in a sense it was the very success of the regime, coupled with the tremendous influx of gold from the recently discovered Californian and Australian deposits (most of which ended up in France), which made uncontrolled investment difficult to check at a time when money was readily available [20; 44].

The dominant economic philosophy of the regime was that of Saint-Simonianism, a mode of socioeconomic thought which had greatly influenced Napoleon III in his youth and which was held by many, including some in his entourage, to be the key to increased prosperity and the means to end incipient class war. One aim of this school of thought was, it was hoped, being realised by the social policies; the other would be achieved by pursuing certain economic policies.

Basically the Saint-Simonians believed that the answer to a lack of steady economic growth was a managed and directed expansion, which presupposed a close collaboration between government and capitalists. The failure of the government of Louis-Philippe to provide this, and the bitter experience of the 1840s, which had seen financial and economic collapse, were undoubtedly factors in the calculations of those who had supported Louis Napoleon and who looked for different results from his government. They were not to be disappointed [*Doc. 7*].

The key to expansion was seen to be mobility, and the key to mobility lay in railway construction. Hence from 1852 to 1860 an unprecedented programme of railway construction was launched with government support. The stimulus this provided was reflected not only in increased investment, but also in increased employment. The construction of the lines required a large and skilled workforce, while the need for locomotives, rolling stock, rails, etc., made demands on the iron and steel industries which led to parallel increases in their workforce and output. In the 1840s French entrepreneurs had found it necessary to use English engineers and imported materials, in order to construct the few railway lines which the period produced. By the 1850s the railways were built using 'home produced' experience and material, at the same time creating one of the finest networks in contemporary Europe. Given that the Saint-Simonians saw France's role in the Mediterranean as being of primary importance, in that she would have easier access to Algeria, the linking of Northern France with the Mediterranean was one of the major achievements. This north-south link not only gave the whole country access to the trade of North Africa and the Near East, but it made Marseilles the fastest growing city in the Empire and a real centre of Mediterranean trade.

The building of the Suez Canal, a project which a French company began in 1859, was an extension of this financial-commercial penetration of the Near and Middle East and was envisaged as providing France with an opportunity to play an important role in Far Eastern affairs. The same drive for railway expansion also linked France to the whole continent, while the activities of French companies and French banks in other European states such as Italy and Spain were an indication of her growing economic and financial strength [54; 56].

The effects of railway growth on the domestic economy were, if less spectacular, of no less importance. The opening up of whole regions to swift and efficient transport encouraged a growth in agriculture because new markets were now available for the sale of produce, while the transportation of fertilisers in bulk made possible the growing of new crops in areas which had hitherto been unable to support them because of soil deficiencies.

All this led to an increase in rural prosperity which not only helped to popularise the regime with the peasantry but produced tangible changes, for the first time, in the mode of life of the *mass* of the population. The government did its best to encourage investment in agriculture, so that the economy should not become unbalanced by an overconcentration on industrial growth, though the effects were less sensational, for the return on investment was less tempting.

Nevertheless, by insisting that the railway concessionaires be responsible for improving the land through which their railways ran, by drainage and by afforestation, private enterprise was made to assist in rural development. The regime itself, by pursuing the same programme combined with road and bridge building, ensured a steady increase in the opening up of the country as a whole. The founding, under government impetus, of agricultural and veterinary colleges, as a specialised feature of the encouragement of education in general, was in the nature of a long-term investment in the future of agricultural development, but the use of trained agronomists together with the introduction of farm machinery was already having an effect on crop yields before 1870. For example, in 1848 the wheat harvest had been 87 million hectolitres, while in 1869 it reached 127 million.

The changes which increased prosperity brought to the countryside must not, however, be exaggerated. Life for the majority of the peasantry remained hard and often brutal. But there was *relative* progress, which was what mattered to contemporaries, and the 'great isolation', which had dominated the countryside since time immemorial, was being broken – a fact underlined by the continuing spread of French as a spoken language, replacing *patois* or even established languages such as Breton and Provençal. Thanks to its opening up of communications and a vigorous education policy, the Second Empire was to make great progress in the creation of a unified nation. Here again, however, one must not exaggerate: in 1864 a report on primary education noted: 'Despite all efforts the French language spreads only with difficulty' [58].

The difficulty in establishing a national language throughout France was a clear indication to the government of the necessity for a programme of mass education – particularly as the adult male population was now enfranchised. In theory this should have been a simple matter of providing schools and teachers, but in practice the problem was more complex. The reason was that the Church, by no means a negligible factor in the provision of education, contested the right of the state to usurp what it felt was its traditional role. These conflicting claims had resulted in a constant battle over who should exercise control over the educational system. By the time of the Second Empire, a working compromise had been reached: the state system of primary and secondary education was essentially secular in its orientation while, alongside it, the Church had established, in parallel, schools in which traditional religious teaching was an integral part of the curriculum. This situation had come about because the conservative classes, casting about for explanations as to why there had been a 'red' revolution in 1848, decided that the lay teachers in the schools were in many ways the culprits. They had preached socialism in the classrooms, and the only antidote to this poison was to allow the clergy to teach 'moral' values. As part of the general conservative reaction after 1848, the Falloux Law, passed in 1850, authorised the opening of schools outside the state system. In theory this meant any group could benefit from the new law, but in practice it meant only the religious congregations whose vocation was teaching.

Until 1860 the Church was able therefore to pursue a policy of expanding its schools alongside those of the state, but after that date the government began to move towards a policy of greater secularisation in education, a move which soon brought it into conflict with the ecclesiastical establishment. In 1863 the Emperor appointed Victor Duruy as Minister for Public Instruction in spite of, or perhaps because of, the well-known anti-clerical convictions of this distinguished historian. What Duruy envisaged was the creation of a system of free, compulsory and lay education which would put an end to the uneasy cohabitation which at present existed with the Church. Duruy, with the full support of the Emperor, succeeded in establishing the principle of free primary education – though he had to compromise on some of his plans. He also negotiated an increase in the salaries of both men and women primary teachers, making teaching a more attractive profession and thus increasing its numbers. As a result of his efforts 8,000 schools opened in the towns and a further 2,000 in the countryside. The curriculum was also revised in order to give it a more 'practical' orientation: there were to be classes in household management for the girls and, for the boys, there were to be introductory courses in technical subjects.

Not content with reforming education at primary and secondary levels, Duruy encouraged the growth of adult education. So successful was this programme that by 1869 there were over 800,000 enrolments – including 100,000 girls and women.

The bulk of Duruy's reforms met with hostility from churchmen – which was to be expected, since they directly threatened the Church's educational structure. However, church leaders found support among the lay conservatives to whom mass education without 'religion and morality' remained an object of dislike and suspicion. The answer to this opposition came from the Emperor himself who said, 'In a country with universal suffrage, every citizen must know how to read and write.' What particularly scandalised conservatives, both lay and clerical, was the emphasis laid by Duruy on the education of females. The clergy denounced the schools, reminding the parents of the risks to which their daughters would be exposed. The idea that girls might be taught by men, as opposed to nuns, was held in especial horror – 'a thing unheard of in the history of civilisations'. Duruy remained unmoved by all this clamour, encouraged by the public gesture of support given by the Empress Eugénie who sent her nieces to attend the classes organised for girls.

When in 1869, Duruy left his post as a result of the ministerial reshuffle that year, he had successfully carried through a programme of reforms ranging from the university to the primary school which was to influence the direction of educational policy in France for the next sixty years.

THE REFORMS OF THE 1860S

It can be conceded that, on the whole, the economic and social problems of the country were approached seriously by the government of Napoleon III. It can further be conceded that, by and large, the regime could show a considerable credit balance in terms of what it had achieved. Yet it certainly cannot be conceded that much gratitude was shown in return for the progress made. It is true that the peasantry were certainly loyal and, in contrast to earlier periods, quiescent, but the workers remained restive, while at the level of the higher industrial and commercial interests the regime faced bitter criticism and hostility. Paradoxically, it seemed that the class which most stood to benefit, and indeed *did* benefit, from the regime, also provided its most bitter opponents.

The reasons for this hostility were rooted in the political and economic situation which the Second Empire inherited but which, in turn, was aggravated by the policies pursued by Napoleon III. The structure of the French economy in the first half of the nineteenth century was based largely on control by private family groups, not open to external investment, who wished to keep control of industrial growth within their own circle. It should not be imagined that this had seriously retarded the growth of industry, but it had both limited it and made it in some ways overcautious. The influence of the great banking houses, in particular that of the Rothschilds, was exercised in favour of this closed circle of economic development and this tended to give the banks too great an influence on the direction and form of growth. Furthermore, one of the basic tenets of this group was that French industries needed protection [20; 34; 59].

Napoleon III was resolved on two things. First, the democratisation of capital, and second, the introduction of free trade, both of these ideas being inherent in the thinking of the Saint-Simonian school of economics. Apart from economic considerations, the Emperor also saw these moves as part of his political programme, in that increased opportunities for investment would broaden the base of the regime financially, as well as providing a greater flow of capital. As for free trade, he considered it to be a means of cheapening the cost of living and thereby benefiting the masses. From a longer term viewpoint, he also hoped that free trade would promote pacific policies among nations.

The policy of the government was therefore to encourage new forms of banking which would be more flexible and directly linked to the needs of industrial growth. Napoleon III found support from the Péreire brothers, convinced Saint-Simonians themselves, who set up the famous *Crédit Mobilier* designed to produce the cash flow that industry needed. They achieved their aim by the simple device of interesting the small saver in the prospects of interest paid on a modest investment. They rejected the image of the great 'temples of money' and took the magic out of banking by making its resources available to everyone with money to invest. For its part, the government negotiated direct loans by public subscription, bypassing the great banking houses and again demonstrating that there was a considerable reserve of capital readily available in the hands of small investors, who would part with their money providing they were certain of a stable political situation which would guarantee their investment.

It was precisely this type of financial operation which was so much resented by the conservative bankers, who blamed the *Crédit Mobilier* and all its works for producing the atmosphere of speculative frenzy which seemed to threaten not only morals, but also monetary stability. Behind this lay a political conviction that involvement in credit and investment should be limited to those sections of society best able to understand it and profit from it. So a great deal of time and energy was deployed in verbal attacks on the 'new' finance, not perhaps in themselves dangerous, but when they were combined with financial manoeuvres to overthrow the rival establishments, they proved lethal. By the 1860s 'orthodox finance' was triumphing once again, and by 1867 it had broken the power of its rivals [58].

It had achieved this victory because after 1860 it found powerful allies in the business interests who were scandalised by Napoleon III's free-trade policies. The signing of the commercial treaty with Britain in 1860, the most important of a series concluded in the next two years, produced a flood of criticism of the high-handed way in which the Emperor had behaved. It was dubbed 'an economic *coup d'état*', to put it on a par with that of 2 December 1851, and its immediate effect was to produce a concerted and dangerous attack upon the regime. Since the treaty, far from making France a free-trade area, simply made it less protectionist, the hostility it aroused clearly sprang from political as much as economic motives.

Certainly not all French manufacturers reacted so sharply; many welcomed the opportunity given to expand in the face of competition. But the opponents made common cause with other groups in a 'coalition of discontent' made up of political conservatives, disgruntled bankers, and others disaffected to the regime. It was a dangerous mixture, not least because the people involved were frequently in positions of power and responsibility who, from this vantage point, were able seriously to attack the Emperor. They forced changes in the financial structure not only in the matter of tighter budgetary control, but also in obliging Napoleon III to abandon those sections of the constitution which enabled him to raise state loans without recourse to the Legislative Body.

In December 1861 the appointment of Achille Fould, a member of one of the great, traditional banking families, as Minister of Finance was seen by contemporaries to mark a definitive change in policy. The triumph of political and financial Orleanism, as this type of conservatism had come to be designated, also marked a turning point in the history of the Empire. As one historian has said: 'The role of the Emperor was finished. More and more the "modern ruler" was going to become a nuisance'. Fould's comment was more succinct: '*Il faut se débarrasser de lui*' ('It's time to get rid of him') [58]. The problem of 1848–51 was, in fact, reasserting itself: could Napoleon III be made to rule under constraint as had been the case in 1848–9 when Barrot and the Orleanists had tried to control him? Or could he be done without altogether? Now that the Emperor had created an apparently prosperous and stable society, it seemed there was no longer any need to keep him there – unless he 'behaved himself'. The Emperor was equally aware of the problem, and applied himself to developing new directions. Clearly, the reforms of 1860–61 were an indication that he realised the necessity to reaffirm his position by bringing the government more directly into contact with the Chamber. At the same time he hoped to disarm a portion of his critics by being one step ahead of them. This he had indeed achieved, since no one expected the reforms. Although the press was controlled, it was not mute, and the reactions of the opposition press revealed clearly the disarray into which the Emperor's reforms had thrown them [72]. As one opposition newspaper put it: 'If we sum up the implications of these important reforms ... against the modest hopes which we entertained we are tempted to say that they have certainly gone beyond those hopes'. There was no doubt that in the political game Napoleon III had taken a neat trick. The opposition groups had not expected that the Emperor would make concessions, and, apart from the implications of his action in the short run, they served as a reminder of the promise made to liberalise gradually; 'Liberty crowns the edifice', as Napoleon III had said.

The political effects of the reforms were important in that they produced a greater degree of acceptance of the regime among a section of its opponents. Most noticeably, they produced a breach among the Republicans when Emile Ollivier, one of the most outstanding among them, spoke in the Legislative Body in their favour [53]. It was not the Republicans, however, who mattered in this context, since they were too feeble and too few. The real test would come when the conservative bloc revealed to what extent their opposition had been disarmed. All too soon it became clear that they regarded the reforms as something to be exploited in their interests and that they intended to use them as a basis for further attacks rather than as a means of reconciliation.

The simplest method of attack was, of course, to denounce the reforms as useless, since they neither went far enough nor did they alter the basic features of the regime. What the conservative bloc really wanted was a return to a system of parliamentary government such as had existed under Louis-Philippe. The Orleanists saw themselves as the real ruling class, the only section of society which understood sound government and sound economic policies, and considered that they should therefore have political power. It was precisely this attitude which Napoleon III was determined to combat, because he saw in this desire for a return to parliamentarianism a revival of divisive party politics. Since Bonapartism was essentially non-party (there was *no* official Bonapartist party) and had for its aim the uniting of the national will, the Emperor constantly reaffirmed his determination to avoid any return to a parliamentary form of government. The question was, after the reforms of 1860–61, could he prevent it? One observer thought not: 'His speeches are basically a criticism of the parliamentary regime, yet it is precisely towards this regime that he is being dragged without his seeming to be aware of it'.

In view of this, the elections of 1863, which would produce the third elected body of the reign, were of great importance to both government and opposition.

As often happens in similar circumstances, both groups claimed a victory in the elections. Napoleon III, in his speech from the Throne to the Chambers, remarked that: '… for the third time, in spite of some local disagreements, I can only congratulate myself on the results. You have all sworn the same oath; that is the proof of your co-operation'. Oath or not, it was clear from the elections that there was a resurgence of older ideas. Men like Thiers, who had not been seen since December 1851 and who was the archetypal representative of Orleanist parliamentarianism, reappeared in the Chamber, while the Republicans increased their representation from five to fifteen. Apart from these more or less declared opponents, there were representatives of the anti-free-trade lobby, as well as a group of 'political Catholics'. These latter were made up of those who resented the aid given by Napoleon III to the movement for

Italian unity – aid which had brought down on the Emperor the wrath of Pope Pius IX. Significantly, the protectionists and the Catholics made common cause, though they had little in common apart from their determination to oppose the regime. The government, however, had a clear majority in the Chamber, and for the moment this majority appeared to be sufficiently homogeneous to ensure that the regime could hold to its course. The danger lay in the fact that the majority was liable to fragment if government policies were not to its liking, since many of the deputies opposed any further reforms which they saw as a threat to the whole structure of government [44; 52]. The opposition, well aware of this, adopted a tactic of constant skirmishes rather than mounting an all-out assault, in the hope that the majority would crumble. They were lucky in that events both at home and abroad provided them with ammunition for their attacks.

CRISIS AND RE-FOUNDING 1866–70

For the first time since the establishment of the regime, personalities (other than that of Napoleon III himself) became important, because the question of guiding and controlling the Legislative Body became a critical issue. Given the fact that the Chamber now contained men who had cut their political teeth in the parliamentary assemblies of Louis-Philippe, and who knew the tricks of their trade, it was essential that the Emperor find ministers who could outwit these tacticians.

Unfortunately for Napoleon III, his choice of ministers was circumscribed by factors he could not control. In 1863 came the sudden death of Billault, a man with a 'parliamentary' background, but one who was totally loyal to the regime. As a Minister without Portfolio and then as Minister of State, he had already given good service both in the Legislative Body and outside it. Clearly, in circumstances where 'parliamentary' ability was required, he would have been invaluable, and indeed Napoleon III, writing to the Empress, described his loss as 'irreparable'.

A further blow came in 1865 with the death of the Duc de Morny, the Emperor's illegitimate half-brother, who had been President of the Legislative Body since 1854. Morny, who had been one of the leading movers in the organisation of the *coup* of 2 December, had, through family and business interests, always remained closely linked with the Orleanist groups. Nevertheless, he had faithfully served Napoleon III, even though it was clear that his

Orleanist past made him incline to a more liberal, if not necessarily parliamentary, regime. Because he straddled both political worlds, as it were, together with the fact that he was a man of great political subtlety and finesse, Morny had been ideal as 'manager' of the Legislative Body, and for eleven years he had fulfilled this role with great skill. His death could not have been more inopportune, not only because no one else was as capable of controlling the Chamber but also, and more important for the future, because it was Morny who had understood the attitude of the Republican deputy, Emile Ollivier, in 1861. Ollivier, the son of a well-known Republican who had been proscribed and exiled in December 1851, had remained attached to Republican ideals, and had been elected a deputy in 1857 as an opposition candidate. He was, however, disposed to accept the Empire, provided it was prepared to concede liberty, and he had therefore welcomed and accepted the reforms of 1860–61. This had led to a breach with his Republican colleagues, who feared that Ollivier was selling out to the regime [53] [*Doc. 8*].

Since that date, Morny had been working to bring Ollivier into closer contact with Napoleon III, knowing that one of the things both men disliked, albeit for different reasons, was the Orleanist/ parliamentary bloc. Ollivier considered that: 'Just as representative government is great, so parliamentary government is contemptible', an attitude which certainly distanced him from the 'liberal' critics of the regime. Although Ollivier had been virtually disowned by the other Republican members, his acceptance of the regime, and his adherence to aspects of the Emperor's policy, led to his being identified as a possible means of reconciling the opposition. Morny, in particular, had seen the value of Ollivier's position, and it was Morny who had made certain that Ollivier should become the man responsible for drafting the law of 1864 which conceded the right to strike. Ollivier's handling of this difficult task not only made clear his ability, but also reinforced the impression that he was willing to work with the regime. Clearly, it was Morny's intention to move Ollivier into a position where he might even be prepared to accept office, providing that the Emperor held to his reform programme. With Morny's death the situation changed sharply.

Faced with the difficulty of keeping the majority in the Chamber together and of managing the government's business in the face of hostile attacks, it was necessary for Napoleon III to find someone who was experienced and able. He made a tentative approach to Ollivier, but the move failed, largely because the Emperor feared that, as minister, Ollivier would be unable to control the Chamber and would simply be an isolated and powerless figure. The Emperor therefore decided to appoint Rouher, one of the most able of the men who had been with him since 1850, and who had been instrumental in drawing up the Constitution of 1852. He, with his friend and colleague Baroche, another of those who had emerged in 1850, were regarded as the 'hard liners' of the ministerial group. As President of the Council of State, Baroche did his best to maintain the Emperor's policy in the face of attacks, but he was not of the calibre of Rouher. Even more importantly, in view of the opposition's attitude, he was not as convinced a free-trader [30; 39].

The appointment of Rouher as Minister of State in 1863 had been the outcome of the nearest thing to a ministerial crisis the Empire had yet produced, because, for the first time, there had been a virtual struggle for office. This in itself was a remarkable indication of how the political situation was changing, since according to the constitution it was the Emperor who appointed his ministers and they were responsible only to him. The fact that Napoleon III was obliged to put up with squabbles among the ministerial group was something new, and although he rode out the crisis by using his peculiar combination of skill and patience, it was a warning that things were not as they had been. Rouher, once installed as Minister of State, set out to do battle with the opposition in order to restore government control of the Chamber. The first challenge came almost immediately, for in January 1864 Thiers presented to the Legislative Body his demands for the introduction of the 'Five Necessary Liberties'. These 'liberties' were, according to their author, liberty of the individual, freedom of the press, electoral freedom (no government-assisted candidates), freedom for the deputies to table amendments to proposed legislation and to question ministers, and, finally, the acceptance of ministerial responsibility. In fact, the programme, if accepted, would have meant a return to the monarchy of Louis-Philippe, although Thiers assured his colleagues that his proposals could be adopted without overthrowing the existing regime. Rouher responded and in a brilliant oratorical performance demolished the idea of the parliamentary programme by recalling the ambivalence of Thiers's political past. If the parliamentary monarchy was such a splendid system, why had he helped to overthrow it in 1848? By his victory over Thiers, Rouher demonstrated to the majority his own ability and reassured them as to the government's determination to avoid a return to Orleanism [*Doc. 9*]. But the real problem was not how to obtain a short-term triumph; rather it was, in the long term, how to sustain and control the majority in the face of continued attack. As the government's position began to weaken both at home and abroad, this task became more and more difficult. In particular, the clear failure of Napoleon III to maintain France's European position in the face of increasing Prussian power after 1866, coupled with the disaster in Mexico, gave great comfort to the opponents of the regime. For the same reasons its supporters fell increasingly into disarray, and it seemed as if Rouher would fail in his attempts to keep control [39].

Ollivier, who was aware of Rouher's difficulties and disliked him personally, decided to make a bid for office. In January 1866, just some six months before the Prussian victory over Austria, he attempted to produce a stable governmental group in the Legislative Body, which would convince the Emperor of its loyalty while at the same time urging him on to reform. To this end forty-two deputies, all well known for their devotion to the dynasty, signed an amendment to the speech from the Throne. It is possible that something might have emerged from this initiative, for it would seem that for a time Napoleon III hoped to bring Ollivier into the ministry with Rouher. Such a combination would have strengthened the government at ministerial level and consolidated a new majority in the Chamber, but any hope that this might occur was unfortunately wrecked by the antipathy between the two men. It was difficult to achieve a reconciliation between Ollivier and Rouher, largely because the latter represented the hard-line approach of the early days of the regime, and was known to be lukewarm (to say the least) towards any further reforms which he considered would be fatal to it. Ollivier, already an isolated figure as a result of his breach with the Republicans, feared that he would simply be swallowed up by becoming a minister, and would lose the support he was so painfully trying to build up. A further problem for Ollivier lay in the fact that a ministerial collaboration with Rouher would deny him any freedom of manoeuvre, and would hopelessly compromise his attempts to build bridges between moderate republicanism and the regime.

On the other hand, it would have been impossible for Napoleon III to take Ollivier as a minister and let Rouher go, for Ollivier was inexperienced, and almost certainly the Legislative Body would have made it impossible for the government to transact its business. The majority, already crumbling even under the control of a tough and experienced minister, would have fallen apart when confronted with Ollivier [43].

So Napoleon III kept Rouher, but forced him to swallow the liberal pill by introducing a programme of reforms. The unfortunate minister found himself presenting to the Chamber two measures of great importance, for neither of which he had any sympathy, because he feared they would fatally weaken the regime. The first measure ended virtually all restrictions on the press, while the second established the right of public meetings to discuss political questions. The effect of both these concessions was to open the door to the expression of critical and oppositionist views without restraint, thus raising the whole level of political awareness among the public. As the public were also the electors, it meant that elections would now be fought more vigorously and openly than since 1851. It was a bold step forward, but as with previous reforms, it produced dissension among the regime's right-wing supporters, because they thought the reforms too sweeping, while for their part the opposition condemned the measures as inadequate.

In the confusion which this situation created, both at the level of ministry and legislature, Napoleon III struggled to get a new military law accepted. The Prussian victory of 1866 over Austria had made it plain that France must face up soon to a crisis with the emerging new European power, and it was equally plain that the crisis might result in war. Napoleon III and his senior military advisers were convinced that the army must be reorganised if it was to be effective.

Basically, the reorganised army would have contained more men, been better equipped with more modern weapons, and been capable of speedy deployment. It would also have cost a great deal more than the present military dispositions of France actually did.

The debate on the army reforms in the Chamber revealed how sharply the government's position had deteriorated since 1863. The 'Left' opposition, basically the Republican group, attacked the plans for an enlarged army on the grounds that it would be 'an instrument of repression and caesarism'. They defended themselves against the charge that by opposing an increase in the army they were weakening France's military position, by clinging to their theory of 'the nation in arms'. It was an article of belief among Republicans that the great victories of the Revolution from 1791 to 1800 had been won by a combination of patriotic fervour and an innate military capacity which the French possessed. In the event of the 'country being in danger' the same spirit would animate the nation. Hence, there was no need for a large standing army. All the government needed to do was to trust, and to arm, the people.

The conservative, Orleanist opposition, as befitted men of sound financial principles, criticised the proposals on grounds of expense. Apart from which, Thiers, as ever their spokesman, thought that the figures which the government had issued about the relative strength of the French and Prussian armies were, in the case of Prussia, exaggerated.

All of this was bad enough from the point of view of Napoleon III and the army. What made it worse was the fact that Rouher himself was hesitant in his defence of the projects in the debates which ensued. Was Rouher revenging himself on his Emperor for having forced him to support the liberal reforms? That *may* have been one element in the composition of his attitude. But a more important reason was that the military reforms were known to be unpopular in the country at large, because they involved wider conscription, longer service, and heavier taxes, and there would have to be a general election in 1869. No group, including the ministers, wished to face the electorate with a record of having supported the unpopular measures, and so, though for different reasons, each justified its self-interest behind a façade of principle. What is particularly noteworthy, as indicating the increasing limitations on Napoleon III's power, is that Rouher should have been able to justify his half-hearted support for the military reforms by pointing out the damage they could do to governmental candidates in the forthcoming election [39; 44].

As a consequence of this attitude, the Emperor and his War Minister, Marshal Niel, were forced to abandon the main points of the reform programme, although the Chamber was grudgingly persuaded to accept a period of longer military service. The plans for creating a trained reserve body, which would produce 400,000 men immediately on mobilisation, were, however, so hacked about by the Legislative Body as to deprive the force of any real potential. When war came in 1870, this reserve group, known as the *Garde Mobile*, proved more of a menace to internal order than to the external enemy.

Rouher had warned the Emperor that the changes in the press laws and in the laws regarding the holding of public meetings would mean that the elections of 1869 would be quite different in tone from the preceding ones of 1852, 1857 and 1863. That had, indeed, been one of the reasons why he feared the consequences of the military reforms. The break-up of the majority in the Chamber would further mean that there would also be a new balance of political groups in the new Legislative Body. In January 1869, in his last speech from the Throne before the dissolution, Napoleon III stressed the achievements of the regime in its twenty years of existence. He ended by expressing his confidence in the nation, which in the elections would undoubtedly once again reject revolution while voting for the union of authority and liberty. By speaking in this way, the Emperor clearly hoped to reassure the voters of his determination to remain firmly in control, while at the same time indicating to them his determination to pursue his policy of liberalisation.

It would not be an easy task. Already, the liberty of the press had degenerated in many instances into licence, and had reduced the ministers to both anger and despair. At one point Napoleon III had consulted Rouher as to the possibility of proceeding against newspapers by legal action (as happens in Britain), but the latter made it plain that this would rarely work. With a certain grim satisfaction he pointed out that this was precisely why he had been opposed to the removal of the Press Laws, and that the consequences were inevitable. Rouher was not totally correct in his analysis of the weakness of legal proceedings against the press. Henri de Rochefort, a broken down aristocrat of advanced radical views, produced a newspaper called *La Lanterne* specialising in political satire [*Doc. 10*]. The author did not, however, confine himself to politics but also made personal attacks on the Imperial family. This campaign reached its climax when Rochefort, in one issue of the paper, called the Empress a 'crowned whore'. The government could not allow this to go unpunished, but was now deprived of legal means of muzzling the press. The only way to silence Rochefort was by a government prosecution on a legal technicality[38]. Rochefort was accused of having assaulted a printer who had published articles against him, and was sentenced to three years' imprisonment. He fled to Brussels (having been condemned *in absentia*) and from there continued to write hostile pamphlets and articles which were smuggled into France. More serious was the opposition press campaign waged in favour of an obscure deputy, Baudin, who had been killed in December 1851 while attempting to persuade Parisian workers to fight in the streets. Newspaper articles in favour of Baudin were really attacks on the *coup d'état* of December 1851 and on Napoleon III. Significantly, they came not only from the Republican but also from the Orleanist press, and the government's anger was increased by the open unwillingness of magistrates to proceed against offending journals. The conservative nature of the magistrature was revealed by a head-on clash between the Minister of Justice and the Imperial Procurator in Toulouse, who had refused to prosecute an Orleanist newspaper in that city. Only when formally ordered to proceed against the newspaper did the Procurator take action. This campaign, which involved the opening of a public subscription to erect a monument to Baudin, became so violent that the government finally moved in to prosecute Delescluze, one of the main protagonists. The trial of Delescluze, a diehard radical who had spent all his life engaged either in political or journalistic Republicanism of an advanced kind, became, thanks to his lawyer Gambetta, an attack on the regime as a whole. The presiding judge permitted Gambetta to launch a veritable diatribe against the 2 December and upon everything that had happened subsequently, and although Delescluze was found guilty and fined, the affair did much to stir up old resentments [*Doc. 11*].

Gambetta represented the new and vigorous Republicanism of the generation which had grown up under the Empire. Less Utopian and more opportunist than the generation of 1848 (Gambetta had taken the oath and sat in the Legislature), they were nevertheless filled with a deep and passionate dislike of the existing regime. Socially, however, they remained conservative, a fact which weakened their position, in that they carefully avoided involving themselves with working-class agitation. This gap was filled by the more extreme radical Republicans who preached a violent, if unfocused, revolutionary creed of which Gambetta said: 'I will use it as a weapon but alter their aim'. One of the ways in which he, and others close to him, did use it was by linguistically identifying with the group while having serious reservations about its programme. Later on, under the Third Republic, this same tactic was to be pursued with the cry of 'no enemies on the Left'.

In 1868–9, however, the regime was sufficiently strong to ride out the storm, but only because Napoleon III had the sagacity to run before the wind. As he wrote to his cousin Prince Napoleon: 'I may founder, but upright and not worm-eaten'. Everything now turned upon the Emperor's ability to deal with the political situation, since no other person was, in the nature of the regime, capable of producing a solution. There were some positive factors. In spite of all the campaigning by the various opposition groups, the government found that the election results were far from adverse [52]. It had still achieved a considerable majority of the votes cast, 1,400,000 over the total for the opposition, and even this figure did not represent the true extent of its victory. The fragmentary nature of the opposition meant that even though it had polled 900,000 more votes than in 1863, its divisions annulled much of its potential strength. A fair evaluation would be to say that although many of the new deputies were not 'government men' they were also, apart from the irreconcilable Republicans, not hostile to the regime as such. What they wanted was a refounding which would maintain the Empire but would remodel the governmental institutions.

Napoleon III was in accord with this view, but, as he had done before in his political career, he decided to let his critics play first in the game. To this end he let the new Chamber present him with a programme, rather than impose one from above. He summoned the Legislative Body for a special session in June 1869 at which the elections of the new deputies would be validated. Such a meeting would give these deputies an opportunity of getting together before the normal session in November, and Napoleon III hoped that they would seize the chance to draw up a programme outlining their projects for reform. This meant that, if all went well, he could confront the opening session of the Chamber in November with a ministry, with a reconstituted majority, and an agreed agenda of reforms.

The plan worked, and in July a group of 116 deputies, with Emile Ollivier as their spokesman, presented their project [11]. All those who signed made it clear that they supported the regime, did not wish to attack the position of the Emperor, and were not associated with either Orleanism or intransigent Republicanism. Napoleon III, having forced the opposition to define its programme, conceded all that was requested, in some instances going beyond the demands of the 116. It was agreed that ministers could be deputies, they would appear in the Chamber, government policy could be debated and, to add to the budgetary control already established, all commercial treaties would have to be ratified by the Legislature. This last provision meant that there would be no repeat of the 'commercial *coup d'état*' of 1860. Perhaps more ominously for the future, it reflected the extent to which the anti-free traders had increased their strength in the new house. Since the free-trade policy had been one of the hallmarks of the regime in its earlier phase, this tilt of the balance in favour of protectionism marked the extent of the economic as well as political changes.

It was clear to everyone that this time, unlike 1867, new policies would require new men. Persigny, one of Louis Napoleon's companions from the early days, wrote to Ollivier: 'The Emperor must continue along the liberal ways he has opened up, but he must summon a new generation of young men, firm and intelligent as well as convinced and courageous. As for the men of 2 December, like me, ... our role is finished'. On 12 July 1869 Rouher, 'burning what he had adored', outlined the new reform programme to the assembled deputies, and that evening he and all the Ministers resigned. The Emperor adjourned the Legislative Body until November, and an interim ministry was appointed to supervise the preparation of the proposed legislation, which had then to be presented to the Senate. As guardian of the constitution, the Senate had to ratify any changes which affected the actual structure of the regime.

Before anything else, however, it was essential to find someone who would be able to work with the Emperor in embarking on the reforms. It could only be Ollivier; first because Napoleon III wanted him, second because this time Ollivier was willing to take office now that Rouher had been removed. Above all was the fact that it now seemed possible that Ollivier, using the '116' as a base, could produce a governmental majority in the Chamber, without which the governmental system would be unworkable.

Negotiations began between the two men in November, but dragged on because Ollivier was determined that the new ministry should represent a complete break with the past and should contain no former ministers. Napoleon III, concerned to maintain continuity because it also represented experience, wanted Ollivier to keep one or two men from the previous administration. It may also be that Napoleon III hoped to mollify the diehard Bonapartists in the Legislative Body by keeping a vestige of the more authoritarian structure. The corollary of this must be that they would, unwillingly, be compelled to accept Ollivier and to support him, thus increasing his chances of finding a majority in the Chamber.

Ollivier, for reasons which were comprehensible although not very wise politically, refused all compromise, and finally, in a letter of 27 December, the Emperor gave him full powers to form a ministry 'resolved to apply the *senatus consultum* of 8 September' [*Doc. 12*]. The date referred to was that on which the Senate had ratified ·the reform proposals which, from that moment, had the force of constitutional law [11; 44].

Immediately Ollivier began to search for a ministry he found himself in difficulties. Instinctively, he looked to the signatories of the famous 'Interpellation of the 116' to provide him with his colleagues, but the very diversity which in opposition had seemed its strength, representing as it did so many shades of opinion, now turned out to be a serious weakness. The differences between those among the signatories who were possible ministers proved too great, and Ollivier's first grouping foundered at the last minute because of them. This threw him to the 'wolves' of the Legislative Body, where the activities of the parliamentarians had increased in parallel with Ollivier's difficulties, and where the influence of Thiers was all-important. The 'Ministry of 2 January', as it came to be called, was indeed so 'parliamentary' in tendency that Thiers said of it: 'The opinions which I represent are seated on the ministerial bench'. Or as another critic put it: 'It was the successor to Guizot's ministry after a lapse of twenty years'.

It seemed to contemporaries that in trying to create a liberal Empire, Napoleon III had merely succeeded in destroying everything he had hoped to create, by opening the door to a parliamentary regime resembling that of the Orleans Monarchy (1830–48). The effect of this was to make all interested parties determined to define what exactly Napoleon III's position now was. This explains the constitutional struggle which lasted from January until April 1870, and which turned basically upon a definition of the Emperor's power under the new system.

It soon became clear that there was no simple solution to the problem of the balance of authority, and the constitution of 1870, as it finally emerged, seemed likely to rival the much despised constitution of 1848 in its consolidation of apparent contradictions. The key weakness was the creation of dual responsibility by making the ministers answerable to both the Legislative Body and the sovereign. This was a deliberately chosen contrivance, since it seemed the only means of preventing the new system degenerating into a pure parliamentary monarchy in which the ministers issued from, and were responsible to, the Chamber. In that sense the creation of a dual authority represented a clear rejection of 'Orleanism', a rejection reinforced by the provision that the Emperor would himself be President of the Council of Ministers, thus exercising control over the making of policies. As an ultimate affirmation of executive power, the Emperor was declared to be, as before, responsible to the French people 'to whom he has always the right of appeal'. The question of sovereignty was therefore placed outside any possibility of parliamentary interference, so that the dynastic continuity was preserved and, as Bonapartist theory would have it, this would enable the Emperor to interpret the will of the people. This maintenance of the plebiscitary system was disliked intensely by all those who had hoped to institute a more parliamentary regime. They saw in it, quite rightly, a counterbalance to all they hoped to achieve by making the Legislative Body the real power, in which the deputies represented the people's will. In an attempt to circumvent the implications of this, they proposed that a plebiscite should be held to ratify the constitutional changes, but that it should be authorised by the Chamber. Such a move was not only in defiance of the constitution but also represented a direct attack on the Emperor's position. The Emperor, who had at first been against holding a plebiscite, dished his opponents by agreeing that there should be one, but that the Legislative Body should have no part in it [*Doc. 13*].

In May 1870, a plebiscite was therefore held to enable the nation to ratify the new constitution. The results were a resounding victory for the Emperor and his policies: 7,257,379 voted 'Yes' and 1,530,000 voted 'No'. Gambetta, who as a leading Republican was no partisan of the regime, conceded that 'the Emperor is stronger than ever'. But the victory destroyed the fragile ministry which Ollivier had constructed with such difficulty. The more 'parliamentary' of his colleagues would not stomach what seemed to be an end to their hopes for an increase in the power of the Legislative Body and resigned, leaving Ollivier to construct a new ministry. After great difficulties he did manage, with the support of Napoleon III, to put together a new grouping, but the new ministry proved to be no stronger than the old one and soon found itself confronted with serious problems.

In the Chamber the authoritarian Bonapartists, who had never liked the drift towards a more liberal interpretation of the constitution, had interpreted the victory in the plebiscite as a reaffirmation of the Emperor's personal power, and they now renewed their attacks on Ollivier. The Republicans showed little desire to support their one-time colleague while the 'centre', led by Thiers, concentrated on forcing Ollivier to compromise with them in order to push their own interests. In 1869 Ollivier had hoped to bring about a reconciliation, but he had clearly underestimated the extent of the political rancour and irresponsibility which members of the Legislative Body possessed.

He seemed more and more to depend on luck and Napoleon III's support for his maintenance in office, and in this difficult situation he was confronted with the most serious crisis which had ever affected the regime – that of the Hohenzollern Candidacy and the threat of war with Prussia. Given the fact that Bismarck was resolved on provoking a war, as he admitted twenty years after the event, it would have been difficult for any French government to avoid falling into the trap. What made the crisis of July 1870 so dangerous was the confusion and weakness which dominated all the moves made in Paris and which obviously reflected the weakness of the ministry. Certainly, the result of the first stage of the crisis, the withdrawal of the Hohenzollern Candidacy in Spain, was a great diplomatic victory for France; but the bellicosity of the public in general, and the desire of the ministry to bolster up its popularity both with the Chamber and with the people at large, led to the 'demand for guarantees' which saved Bismarck from losing the game [18]. The request that the King of Prussia should publicly guarantee that the Hohenzollern candidature would never be renewed was more a blunder than a crime. What was alarming was the manner in which it was organised by Napoleon III, acting directly with the Foreign Minister Gramont, without any previous cabinet discussion, a proceeding which revealed clearly the dangers of the concept of dual responsibility. It was not only constitutional uncertainty, however, which brought about this move; it was also fear of what would happen in the Legislative Body which influenced Gramont's action. He told the British Ambassador: 'The government could not last if it went before the Chamber tomorrow without having received some specific concession on the part of Prussia'. The Ambassador for his part reported to the Foreign Office that: 'In this affair the French government was less at the head of the Nation than following it' [18].

As a result of the decisions taken in such a confused atmosphere, Benedetti, the French Ambassador, had his meeting with the King of Prussia at Ems, the meeting which gave Bismarck the chance to produce his famous 'Ems Telegram'. The original telegram from the King to Bismarck had been innocuous, but the effect of the publication in the French newspapers of Bismarck's *edited* version, making it seem as if the King had insulted the ambassador, produced an upsurge of war fever in France. Desperately anxious to avoid war, Napoleon III, backed by Ollivier and the ministry, suggested a European congress to settle the matter, but it was too late. The newspapers, freed from all control since 1868, whipped up a chauvinistic war fever, while in the Chamber the deputies demanded action, a demand which Ollivier and his ministers felt they dared not resist if they were to survive in office. On 15 July Ollivier made a statement in both the Legislative Body and the Senate which virtually put France in a state of war with Prussia, though the actual declaration came on 19 July. Ominously, for both the ministry and the country, there had already been an attempt by members of the Legislative Body on 18 July to unseat Ollivier, even though France was now at war [*Doc. 14*]. There were no indications of a willingness to sink political differences for the common good, and the departure of the Emperor for the war zone on 19 July, leaving the Empress as Regent, removed the last stable political influence in a highly volatile situation.

3 FOREIGN POLICY 1848–70

The essential point about the foreign policy of the period is that it represented continuity rather than a new departure. Since 1815 successive regimes in France had pursued the same aim: namely, the overthrowing of the Treaties of 1815. The methods might differ, but the ultimate goal remained the same. In 1829 Polignac, as Chief Minister of Charles X, had sought an alliance with Russia, but the reluctance of the Tsar Nicholas, combined with the fall of the Restoration Monarchy in 1830, precluded any success. During the reign of Louis-Philippe, France had been sharply reminded of her international position when she attempted to interfere to her advantage in Belgium between 1830 and 1832, and in the Near East in 1840–41. On both occasions the 'Waterloo coalition' had made threatening diplomatic noises which had led French governments to abandon an adventurous foreign policy in favour of a more restrained approach. This apparent pusillanimity in matters of foreign affairs had helped to make the Orleans Monarchy unpopular and had played its part in the events of 1848.

THE BASIS OF NAPOLEON III's POLICY

With the advent of a Bonaparte to power it was both hoped and expected that France would play a more positive role in European affairs and that, above all, she would be freed from the tutelage in which she had been held since 1815. Louis Napoleon was well aware of what was expected of him. He was also well aware of the risks which a 'forward' foreign policy would entail. The Treaties of 1815 certainly irritated French governments but they did, paradoxically, protect France from the threat of further change, since they rested on an equilibrium accepted by all the major European Powers. It was therefore unlikely that France would be threatened by a major international upheaval, providing that she herself did not provoke it. This explains Napoleon III's famous 'The Empire means peace' statement in 1852, which was designed to reassure the French nation and Europe at large that it had no intention of recreating the wars of the First Empire. As one historian of the period has remarked, 'The Emperor gave new drive and direction to French foreign policy ... but he was never in any position to refashion the international order in conformity with his "Napoleonic Ideas" ' [31, p. 73].

The Emperor was resolved to achieve the unpicking of the 1815 system by means of diplomacy rather than war, and to this end he maintained two basic principles of conduct in foreign affairs. The first was an alliance with England, which he considered essential in order to avoid France being isolated in Europe. Napoleon III was convinced that England held the key to future developments on the continent, and he also believed that her commercial, financial and external interests coincided with those of France. The important thing was to make English statesmen see this and accept it, so that a real working entente could be established between the two countries [*Doc. 15*].

The second basic factor in Napoleon III's strategy, which was linked both to his desire for peace and to close collaboration with England, was his belief in the settling of affairs by means of international congresses of the Powers. Here disputes and problems could be solved by discussion and by negotiation. The Emperor believed it possible that states would come together in a 'peace conference' without passing through the intermediate stage of war. To him it seemed that a diplomatic crisis need not necessarily end in armed conflict, but could be resolved by common sense and concession destined to serve the common good of all. It was certainly a laudable doctrine, but in the context of the time it was fairly unrealistic, and a cynic might well have said that had France been militarily more powerful, her ruler would have been less pacific. That is as may be; what seems certain is that Napoleon III *did* try to make his diplomacy work in this way, which accounts for the hesitations and apparent inconsistencies of many of his efforts.

THE CRIMEAN WAR

The first example of this new approach was the Crimean War of 1854–6. Napoleon III has frequently been accused of launching a European war on a flimsy and frivolous pretext, namely France's right to certain privileges connected with the 'Holy Places' in Palestine. The accusation is erroneous for the simple reason that the Emperor chose what he called 'the ridiculous affair of the Holy

Places' precisely because he thought it impossible that it *could* lead to a war [43]. What he sought was a diplomatic *coup* in consort with England in an area where he felt certain that the London government would see the country's interests as being involved. Given that Russia had become the bogey-man of the Foreign Office, Napoleon III felt reasonably certain that in a diplomatic crisis with Russia he could count on support from London. Nicholas I, who considered that the protection of Christians in the Ottoman Empire was his affair, resented the interference of Napoleon III, and his hostile reaction to French policy led to the moving of a joint Franco-British fleet into the Bosphorus as an indication of solidarity between London and Paris. Nicholas retaliated by occupying the two principalities of Moldavia and Wallachia (present day Romania), which were part of the Sultan's dominions. So far nothing had happened to make war inevitable, and in July 1853 Napoleon III organised the Vienna Note, signed by Britain, Prussia and Austria. Conciliatory in tone, it nevertheless represented a triumph for Napoleon III, in that this time not France but Russia was the isolated power in Europe. The Note was designed to reconcile the interests of France and Russia over the question of the Holy Places and would, it was hoped, lead to a more general settlement of the problems within the Turkish Empire on a basis of international cooperation. Clearly, the Emperor assumed that in the circumstances the Tsar would yield to the combined pressure of the Powers; France would thereby have gained her point, and Napoleon III could claim a diplomatic victory. As it turned out, this assumption was correct, for Nicholas did not in fact reject the note, and all might well have ended peacefully had there been time for further diplomatic discussions.

Unfortunately, these calculations were thrown into disarray by the action of the Sultan who, infuriated by the Russian occupation of the principalities, declared war on the Tsar (apparently on his own initiative) in October 1853. The consequences were catastrophic. In the same month, reacting to the Turkish declaration of war, the Russian fleet annihilated the Turkish Black Sea fleet at Sinope and with one blow put the Ottoman Empire virtually at the mercy of the Tsar. In Britain an hysterical press campaign, fed by an endemic Russophobia, clamoured for war against Russia, the perpetrator of the 'Massacre of Sinope'. The fact that the Sultan had brought the disaster on himself was conveniently forgotten.

Suddenly Napoleon III became aware that his plans were falling in ruins, and in an attempt to recover the situation he made a direct appeal to Nicholas to end the hostilities with Turkey. Diplomatically, Russia still remained isolated, and so it was hoped in Paris that a conciliatory approach could still prevent the disaster of an international war [*Doc. 16*].

But Nicholas would not yield, estimating that he had been needlessly provoked and was in the right, and so in March 1854 France, allied to Britain, found herself at war. The only consolation for Napoleon III, now engaged in a war he had not wanted, was that France and Britain were fighting side by side in a common cause. What was more, Britain was swept by a rare wave of Francophilia which manifested itself in the state visits of the respective sovereigns in 1854 and 1855. To that extent Napoleon III could feel that something had been achieved. What was less satisfying was the negative attitude of both Austria and Prussia, who showed no inclination to transform their diplomatic support of 1853 into a military commitment. The only European state to join in on the side of France and Britain was the kingdom of Piedmont, whose Chief Minister, Cavour, had reasons of his own for wanting to have his country noticed internationally. As the war dragged on it was found to be costly, badly managed and increasingly unpopular in France. The Emperor, always sensitive to public reactions, began to look for a way to end the conflict, a desire which led him into difficulties with Palmerston, who was now in control of the government in London and whose Russophobia was legendary.

Fortunately, the death of Nicholas I in March 1855 brought to the throne Alexander II, who was desirous of ending the conflict, even if, to protect his father's honour, he could not immediately initiate peace moves. A renewed diplomatic campaign, once more supported by Austria and Prussia, enabled the new Tsar to ease himself out of the situation and in March 1856 a formal Peace Conference was held in Paris.

On the surface, the Conference was a triumph for Napoleon III, not least because France was once more shown to be at the centre of European affairs. Apart from this, the policy of Franco-British collaboration appeared to be an established fact and bore out the Emperor's comment that: 'If other countries are my mistresses, England is my wife'. It was an unfortunate comparison, in that many marriages are subjected to all sorts of strains and stresses and have been known to end in divorce. Furthermore, it is doubtful if the Foreign Office wished to embrace this degree of intimacy. It certainly had no intention of allowing the Paris Conference to turn into a general Congress, reviewing the entire European scene, which was what Napoleon III really hoped for. Indeed, it was what he had wanted in 1852–3, before the war had occurred. To this end he wooed Alexander II, hoping to produce a triple entente between France, Britain, and Russia, but the Tsar was wary and the British Government totally disinclined to go for anything of this nature. In the event, what did happen left Napoleon III in a more difficult position than in 1854.

For Britain, the war had been essentially about curbing Russian activities in the Near East. Not surprisingly, therefore, Clarendon, the representative in Paris, insisted on the neutralisation of the Black Sea and the closing of the Straits to Russian warships as a means of reducing Russian influence in the region to a minimum [*Doc. 17*]. It was quite clear to Napoleon III that he must either support these demands or break with England. At the same time, because the clauses were odious to the Tsar, his acceptance of them would mean the end of French hopes for a reconciliation with Russia. The clauses were accepted, the Tsar was offended, and Britain had thus neatly managed to obtain a hold on French foreign policy. So long as the Black Sea clauses remained, so long would France and Russia remain estranged. On several occasions between 1856 and 1863 Napoleon III attempted to draw Alexander into a formal alliance, but without success. The best that could be obtained was a benevolent indifference to French policy, provided Russian interests were not directly threatened [32].

In the short run the attitude of Russia was both important and beneficial to Napoleon III, in that it did allow him to pursue certain objectives which did not appear to have any immediate effect on Russian interests. It was, therefore, possible for France to consider a more active policy in the Italian peninsula, designed to supplant the dominating influence of Austria which had prevailed since 1815.

THE ITALIAN AFFAIR

Napoleon III's interest in Italian affairs was not based upon some altruistic concept of 'doing good' for Italy. Rather it was a question of further dismantling the 1815 settlement in France's interest, while at the same time assisting the growth of the French economy. The development of the railway system meant that Northern and Central Italy, linked to France by a railway network, could provide new markets as well as fresh opportunities for investment. As was the case with other Mediterranean countries, none of the existing Italian states had sufficient financial resources to undertake on its own the building of a substantial railway network, and French financial resources would therefore be essential [*Doc. 18*]. The only other Power which was intensely interested in Italian railway development was Austria, but lack of finance hindered her attempts to push her projects. In any event, it was the Austrian presence in the Peninsula which was resented by Italian patriots, so that even had Austria had the necessary economic strength, she would still have encountered political difficulties.

There were two main obstacles to implementing the changes which French policy held to be necessary. First, Austria would oppose them as an attack on her position and by implication on the treaties of 1815. Second, the Italian kingdom of Piedmont had plans of its own which involved the annexation of Lombardy and Venetia. However, since Austria held Lombardy and Venetia, and since she opposed any alteration in the established frontiers which had been accepted in 1815, it was clear that French and Piedmontese interests coincided. At the Paris Peace Conference in 1856, Cavour, the Piedmontese Prime Minister, had sounded out Napoleon III as to what he might have in mind for Italy. Cavour obviously hoped that Piedmont's participation in the Crimean War would be favourably contrasted with Austria's neutrality and would lead to some declaration of support for the North Italian kingdom. In the event neither France nor Britain displayed any enthusiasm for Piedmontese projects and Cavour came away empty-handed. He also realised that if Napoleon III was to be galvanised into action some new tactic would have to be devised [12].

Fortunately for Cavour there was something which could be used; the fear of a revolutionary movement in Italy. Ever since the collapse of Mazzini's Roman Republic in 1849 the Republican movement had maintained its agitation for a United Italian Republic 'democratic and social'. The movement was incoherent and ill-organised, but it alarmed *all* the established governments in the Peninsula, and it also alarmed Napoleon III. It was not that the Emperor feared the revolutionary party as such; what he did fear was some repetition of the 1848 fiasco which would enable Austria once more to intervene in Italian affairs, and perhaps enable her to reaffirm her ascendancy over Italy. If the only way to suppress revolution was by Austrian intervention, then the Italian states would be even more inclined to look to Vienna for support. Should France be drawn in again, as she had been in 1848–9 in Rome, then the situation might become dangerous because of possible international ramifications [29].

It was, therefore, in Napoleon III's interests to cut the ground from under the feet of the revolution – a point to which Cavour constantly drew the Emperor's attention. In this respect, the attempt by the revolutionary, Orsini, to assassinate Napoleon III and the Empress Eugénie in January 1858, played into his hands. Orsini's attempt convinced Napoleon III of the danger of revolution, and in the summer he met Cavour at Plombières to draw up a scheme for the remodelling of Italy. The plan which ultimately emerged was limited in scope and aims, but it did offer a solution to the problems of both France and Piedmont [*Doc. 19*]. For Napoleon III there was the opportunity to weaken the revolutionary movement, while for Cavour there was the hope of enlarging the kingdom of Piedmont, even at the price of increased French influence in the Peninsula.

It seems quite certain that once again Napoleon III hoped that he could achieve his aim without actually going to war. The complicated diplomatic manoeuvres between July 1858 and March 1859 bear out this thesis, particularly Napoleon III's attempt to summon a European Congress to deal with the 'Italian Question'. Once again the game of diplomacy without war failed, since no one would accept the fact that there *was* a problem in Italy. As Antonelli, the Papal Secretary of State, remarked: 'The Italian question is simply the desire of Piedmont to extend her dominion in Italy. That question need not exist at all if the Great Powers will simply ignore it' [1 p. 16].

Cavour, however, was determined that the Powers should not ignore it, and Napoleon III, having gone so far, was unable to turn back, particularly since, when he wavered, Cavour threatened to publish the Plombières agreement. So, with one hand tied, Napoleon III carried on as best he could in Paris, seeking a diplomatic solution, while Cavour, in Turin, continued to provoke the Austrians.

It was Austria who broke first under the strain of diplomatic tension by despatching an ultimatum to Piedmont demanding the demobilisation of her army which, as an act of provocation, Cavour had put on a war footing. Since the Plombières agreement had stipulated that Piedmont must be the victim of an Austrian attack in order to be made operable, the ultimatum solved Napoleon III's dilemma and France was able to 'come to Piedmont's aid'.

The outcome of the war which followed revealed how fragile was the basis of cooperation between Napoleon III and Cavour. Although the battles of Magenta and Solferino were technically French victories, and should in theory have led to a further campaign, Napoleon III, to Cavour's fury, negotiated an armistice with Franz-Joseph in July 1859. From France's point of view the armistice was essential because of both the military and diplomatic situation. Militarily, the basic reason was that the Austrian army, though badly mauled, was not defeated, while the French army was ravaged by sickness and had suffered serious losses in battle. If the Austrians consolidated their military position in the famous Quadrilateral of fortresses in Northern Italy, it would take a long and hard campaign to dislodge them. Fortunately for Napoleon III, Franz-Joseph was acutely aware of the economic consequences for Austria if he prolonged the war, and so he, for his part, was also willing to end the fighting.

Diplomatically, Napoleon III was not at all sure of his ground. Prussia had begun to make threatening noises about moving troops to the Rhine to take the pressure off Austria, while Britain was anxious for an end to the conflict. There was also the question of the Pope, whose attitude was openly hostile, and who might launch an appeal to the Catholic Powers to come to Austria's support.

As for the armistice itself, it had, as its basic point, the cession to Piedmont of Lombardy only, while Austria was to keep Venetia. In recompense for not finishing the task he had set out to accomplish, Napoleon III agreed to forgo his original promised reward of Savoy and Nice. Cavour, half-demented by rage, resigned his premiership after a vain attempt to persuade his King, Victor Emmanuel, to continue the war alone.

Once again extraneous events pushed both Napoleon III and Cavour further than they wanted to go, although it may be that Cavour was glad to avail himself of the chance of a vicarious revenge on his ally. Not for him the considerations which had made Napoleon III stop in mid-flight: the weakening of the French army by disease; the repercussions of the war in Europe, where Prussia was threatening to mobilise in support of Austria. All these counted for little with Cavour. Obsessed with a sense of frustration and betrayal, he turned to encouraging those very revolutionary movements he had at one time been so keen to thwart.

Napoleon III could do nothing to prevent the actions of Garibaldi in his conquest of Sicily and Naples, nor could he prevent the upset of the carefully balanced scheme prepared at Plombières. Confronted with a united Italy, minus Rome for which he now became responsible, and Venetia which stayed with Austria, all he could do was reassert his claim to Savoy and Nice. Their annexation by France certainly represented a reversal of the 1815 settlement, but the price had been high. The new Italian kingdom was an unreliable quantity because of what had happened in 1859, and although Cavour died in 1861 his immediate successors showed little enthusiasm for France. As for the Pope, infuriated by Napoleon III's actions and hostile to the new kingdom, he could be counted on to react unfavourably to any further moves the Emperor tried to make in Italy. Since Napoleon III found himself having to protect the Papal States against the pretensions of what appeared to be his creation – for the Italians claimed Rome as their 'natural' capital – his position was both contradictory and invidious. He was, in fact, to carry the problem of the Papacy on his back as long as the Empire lasted, for none of his schemes to lay down the burden were successful. The Italians got their much-coveted capital on 10 September 1870, by which time it had ceased to matter to Napoleon III.

This is, however, to look ahead to an event which was not foreseeable in 1861. To contemporaries it did seem as if France had achieved a victory, even if it was not quite what her ruler had anticipated. Nevertheless, the effects on Europe as a whole were unsettling and Napoleon III's policies had revived old fears about French intentions. Britain, alarmed by what appeared to be a resurgence of French military aggression, cooled in her attitude – though not to the extent of actually breaking the entente. The signature of the Cobden commercial treaty in early 1860 was an indication that in some ways relations between the two countries were as firm as ever. The fact that Napoleon III was willing to abandon French intervention in Syria (1860–61) at Britain's request is a further indication of the way in which cooperation worked. Only one aspect continued to worry Palmerston; the French determination to build the Suez Canal which, it was feared, would greatly enhance France's strategic and economic position in the Mediterranean and Near East and might prove a threat to the trade routes to India. Fears of this sort had indeed been behind the British Government's request that Napoleon III remove his troops from Syria [20].

MEXICO

Perhaps the most extraordinary, and certainly the most unfortunate, result of continued Franco-British cooperation was the decision to intervene in Mexico. The action was agreed upon as a result of discussions about Mexican affairs held between Lord John Russell and Thouvenel, Napoleon III's Minister for Foreign Affairs, in the autumn of 1861. The problem which required a solution was that in Mexico chronic governmental instability had led to the failure of successive regimes to honour the debts which they owed to foreign investors. Half-kept promises had for years irritated European governments, who were being constantly pressured by their respective nationals to make the Mexicans pay up. The crisis finally came in 1861 when Juarez, the latest victor in the perpetual civil war, suspended for two years all payments on foreign debts. It was at this point that Britain initiated the discussions on intervention, since she, together with France, was Mexico's largest creditor.

Napoleon III was anxious to cooperate with Britain, and indeed wished to enlarge the proposed expedition to include Spain. He felt that such an alliance might tie Spain closer to France, opening up possibilities for investment and economic expansion which would give French trade and finance a foothold in the Iberian peninsula. Palmerston, well aware of Napoleon III's interest in Spain, acceded to this idea for the simple reason that he felt that a closer eye could be kept on Franco-Spanish relations if the action was tripartite. As a further inducement to allowing Spain to participate it was estimated that Cuba could be useful as a base for naval operations which would certainly have to form a part of an expedition to Mexico.

In assessing the situation, the two main European participants were influenced by the fact that the Civil War which was now raging in the United States meant that the major North American power had no time to spare in enforcing the Monroe Doctrine. Furthermore, it was held by most European observers that the Confederate States stood a good chance of winning, and if this should be the outcome, then the whole balance in North America would be altered [*Doc. 20*].

Napoleon III was aware that Northern Mexico was suitable for cotton growing, and in view of the threatened cotton famine arising from the American Civil War, which could cause a crisis in the French cotton industry, he hoped to be able to open up an alternative source of supply. The Emperor was further taken with the idea of cutting a canal through the Isthmus of Panama, which he foresaw would be a means of revolutionising world trade by linking the Atlantic and Pacific Oceans.

Clearly, ideas of such a nature would involve more than a temporary expedition to Mexico to recover a debt. They would, and did, imply the establishment of a French presence either directly or through a government which would grant special privileges to

France. The British Government had no intention of committing itself to any such venture but was, in pursuit of its own limited interests, prepared to allow Napoleon III to embark on his policy [43; 44].

Given the degree of wilful or unconscious misunderstanding which existed among the partners concerned, it is amazing that the expedition ever managed to set forth. Such apparent unanimity as there was disappeared the moment the coast of Mexico came in sight, and no sooner had the joint fleet anchored at Vera Cruz than the differences came into the open. The Spanish simply gave up, the British made it plain that they were there in order to overawe the Mexicans and collect the money, and only the French landed in force.

By 1862 Britain had concluded a separate agreement with Juarez and, while indicating that she had no wish to hinder any projects of Napoleon III, withdrew totally from the affair. From then on France remained solely responsible for what happened. Napoleon III, committed to a campaign in a distant country about which he was ill-informed both politically and militarily, sank deeper and deeper into a quagmire which he had completely failed to foresee. None of his political calculations worked. Juarez made a deal with the Americans for supplies of arms and munitions, the Mexican monarchists who had seemed so numerous in Paris were thin on the ground in Mexico, so that the new Emperor, Maximilian, established under the auspices of Napoleon III, found little support in his new Empire. It was clear to all that he would survive only so long as France supported him, and by 1866 Napoleon III had decided that he must withdraw. The victory of the North in 1865 in the American Civil War had altered the balance in the Americas, since the Washington government gave notice of its intention to maintain the Monroe Doctrine, while in the summer of 1866 the victory of Prussia over Austria altered the balance in Europe. Faced with these harsh realities, Napoleon III could no longer have maintained a large and costly expeditionary force in Mexico, even if he had wanted to.

Apart from any general diplomatic considerations, the war had given a weapon to the opposition groups in France itself. Insofar as the press laws permitted, the newspapers which were hostile to the government produced articles attacking the expedition and denouncing its aims and objects. Within the Legislative Body the opposition deputies attacked the war as useless and costly, while at the same time making capital out of the fact that those whom the

French had originally gone to protect in Mexico appeared to consist of shady financiers like the infamous Jecker. Jecker was one of the main claimants against the Mexican Government and it was asserted that he had used his friendship with Morny, half-brother to the Emperor, to press for intervention in Mexico in order to recover his debts, and that this had been the basis of the whole affair. While this was a travesty of what had motivated Napoleon III, there were sufficient grounds for the opposition to make its case, and the mud stuck. As it became clear that the intervention in Mexico was ending in ignominy, criticism mounted and the Emperor's position became more and more uncomfortable. The withdrawal of the French army left the unfortunate Maximilian with no real support and little chance of maintaining himself, and it seemed as if Napoleon III had simply abandoned him to his fate. When in 1867 the news of the shooting of Maximilian at Queretaro by the triumphant Juaristas reached Paris, in the middle of the festivities connected with the Great Exhibition then being held, it was seen as a blow to the honour and prestige of Napoleon III. To many observers it seemed that internal dissension, coupled with an unfavourable international situation, presaged the collapse of the regime. The Emperor himself knew the seriousness of the problems which confronted him, and it was his search for a solution which led him to produce the programme of internal reforms coupled with attempts to reorganise and strengthen the French army. Simultaneously, he struggled to reassert France's European position, which had been seriously weakened by the results of Bismarck's policy [44].

THE CONFLICT WITH BISMARCK AND THE WAR OF 1870

From 1863 onwards France's position in Europe would have been difficult even without the Mexican affair. Once Bismarck had decided that Prussia's interests demanded a restructuring of the Germanic Confederation, it was inevitable that France should be affected. The balance of 1815 (as has already been pointed out) was irksome and frustrating, but it *was* a balance, particularly in Germany, where Austria normally acted as a counterpoise to Prussia. In these circumstances, neither German state had shown any inclination to wish to dominate France, who thus remained in a condition of comparative safety, even if constrained by the 1815 Treaties.

Bismarck, by beginning a process of weakening Austria's position in Germany, was therefore not only altering the equilibrium but confronting Napoleon III with a serious dilemma. Would he, as someone interested in unpicking the 1815 settlement, assist Bismarck in weakening Austria? And, as a secondary but even more important question, would he accept the new structure in Germany once Bismarck had achieved his aim? What Bismarck was resolved upon was that Napoleon III would answer his questions *alone*; that is, France would have no ally to support her if she got into difficulties. To this end he had used the Polish insurrection of 1863 as an excuse to draw closer to Russia, leaving Napoleon III to indulge in irritating but ineffectual protests to the Tsar about events in Poland. Since it was quite clear at St Petersburg that Napoleon III either would not, or could not, agree to any revision of the 1856 settlement, Alexander II was confirmed in his latent hostility to the Emperor by French attitudes over Poland in 1863, and any hopes which might have been entertained in Paris of a Franco-Russian entente were unlikely to be realised.

Reassured by this, Bismarck took his first steps towards altering the structure of the German Confederation, which led to the Danish War of 1864. The war revealed that the Anglo-French entente was enfeebled, since Napoleon III could not persuade Palmerston to accept a joint intervention on behalf of Denmark, in spite of bluster and verbiage on the part of the British Prime Minister. Apart from this evidence of a weakening of the entente, there was the fact that Britain had already shown an indifferent hostility to Napoleon III's attempt to launch, yet again, the idea of a European Congress. Queen Victoria had dismissed the proposals as 'an impertinence' and the government made it clear that its views were similar to the Queen's.

Faced with the impossibility of making a concerted Anglo-French approach to Bismarck, and having failed in his attempt to call a Congress, Napoleon III was left with no alternative but to deal directly with his rival, and in 1865 the two men met at Biarritz. Here, Bismarck sounded out the Emperor as to his reactions in the event of hostilities between Prussia and Austria. Cleverly, he enquired as to what Napoleon III would do if, at the end of such a war, Prussia were to give Venetia to Italy? By making such a suggestion Bismarck played his ace, for Napoleon III seized on the idea of disembarrassing himself of at least a portion of the Italian problem in a manner which would not involve France in a military campaign. So it was suggested that at the end of hostilities Bismarck would 'give' Napoleon III Venetia, and he would then bestow it on Italy; the price, of course, was French neutrality [46] [*Doc. 21*].

'To work for the King of Prussia' is a French proverb which signifies to work for no reward. Clearly this was not what Napoleon III had in mind to do; it seems he may have hoped that Austria, knowing by 1866 that she was threatened by a Prusso-Italian alliance, would cede Venetia to avoid a war on two fronts. This would increase her chances of victory in a war with Prussia to such an extent that it might end in stalemate, and this, in turn, would enable Napoleon III to mediate in German affairs. Dangerous though all this hypothesis was, it came within an ace of success and was only wrecked by the one state Napoleon III had tended to omit from his calculations – Italy. The Italian Government, for internal reasons of its own, refused to accept Venetia without fighting, and so Austria's expressed willingness to cede the province was rendered useless. Bismarck got his war, which ended with the battle of Sadowa in 1866, and by the Treaty of Prague, Austria abandoned all her German interests – a move which Bismarck made permanent by the establishment of a new North German Confederation dominated by Prussia. As far as the cession of Venetia was concerned Bismarck kept his word, even though the Italians had been defeated by Austria both on land and at sea. Napoleon III, however, drew little profit from the occasion, acting merely as a diplomatic broker, since the Italians had to acknowledge that they owed their new acquisition solely to Prussia's victory. The Italian Government felt that it owed the Emperor of the French nothing, and continued to clamour for the withdrawal of French troops from Rome so that it might become the Italian capital.

The new North German Confederation established by Bismarck effectively gave the mastery of Germany to Prussia and so altered the European balance. In Paris, recognition of the implications of the new state of affairs was summed up in the comment: 'It is France which has been defeated at Sadowa'. All that was felt to be unclear was the extent of the defeat, and this Bismarck proceeded to make plain. Realising that Napoleon III had lost the diplomatic initiative, and that he could now only react to events instead of creating them, the Prussian Chancellor resolved to lead the Emperor where he wanted him to go. His task was made easier by the fact that Napoleon III appears to have interpreted Prussia's victory as marking the end of the 1815 settlement and to have hoped that the consequences of this new situation could be turned to France's advantage. It was, however, the realisation that henceforward any policy must be backed by the threat of military force which led to the Emperor's plans for reform of the army. Hence the seriousness of the Chamber's refusal to accept them in their entirety in the debate of 1866–7.

Finding himself thus deprived of the military means to face Prussia as an equal, Napoleon III sought to try to recover his prestige by attempting to purchase the Grand Duchy of Luxemburg. Since 1815 this had been a Prussian outpost on the Rhine, and the Emperor hoped that its acquisition would strengthen France's military and strategic position on her eastern frontier. Although the concept of purchase was inglorious, it had the merit of prudence and would serve to reassure public opinion in France, as well as other European governments, that the Emperor's intentions were peaceful. Bismarck appeared at first to be totally willing to negotiate and indeed went so far as to ask the French Ambassador in Berlin, Count Benedetti, to produce a draft outlining France's desires for 'frontier rectification' on her eastern borders. This draft Bismarck subsequently 'mislaid', and it was not to reappear until July 1870, when it turned up in *The Times* at a moment when it was convenient for him to demonstrate to Europe in general, and Britain in particular, just how scheming and disruptive Napoleon III's foreign policies had been.

That moment, however, lay in the future. In the short term Bismarck suddenly did an about-turn on the Luxemburg affair and exposed the secret negotiations to the North German parliament. Here, he presented Napoleon III's plan as an attempt to subvert the 'German Rhine' and as an affront to German national honour. His action served to create strong anti-French feeling among the South German states, and had the effect of drawing them closer to Prussia. Napoleon III was bitter: 'I trusted Bismarck and he has betrayed me', he confided to the British Ambassador, but there was little he could do and only the diplomatic support of Britain saved him from a total fiasco. Thanks to the activities of the British Ambassador in Paris, who made strong representations to the Foreign Office on the Emperor's behalf, a conference was called in London to settle the Luxemburg question. A compromise was agreed whereby Prussia withdrew her garrison and dismantled the fortifications, while the Duchy was at the same time given an international guarantee of permanent neutrality, as had been done with Belgium [44; 46].

The incident was thus closed, with little profit to Napoleon III, but it represented a turning point in Franco-Prussian relations. Henceforward, the Emperor distrusted Bismarck and was convinced that he would, if necessary, pick a quarrel with France which could lead to war. Bismarck himself was to say in later life: 'The war of

1870 lay in the logic of history', which was a fairly meaningless statement if looked at critically, since 'history' has no 'logic'. What Bismarck might have said with greater truth was that the results of his own policy pushed France into war so that he might bring about the ultimate triumph of Prussia over the other German states.

From 1868 onwards the Prussian Chancellor sought a pretext which would provoke a clash, and in the autumn of that year events in Spain provided him with an opportunity. Queen Isabella had, by a combination of political ineptitude and blatant immorality, so offended the political groups in Spain that she was expelled in October 1868. The generals who had organised the *coup* began the search for a new sovereign, looking for someone who, as Lord Clarendon said, 'would be sufficiently idiotic to want that crown of thorns'. Given the proximity of Spain to France, coupled with the increasing economic interests which now linked the two countries, Napoleon III could not be indifferent as to who might end up on the Spanish throne.

The first potential claimant was the Duc de Montpensier, a son of Louis-Philippe and therefore a representative of a dynasty which was personally offensive to Napoleon III, and whose installation as King might serve also to increase the strength of Orleanist feeling in France. Bismarck tacitly, if indirectly, supported this candidate, knowing it would annoy the French Government, only dropping it when the British Government made it plain that it too did not favour Montpensier. The German Chancellor had no intention of providing any means by which the London-Paris entente might be strengthened.

In the spring of 1869 rumours of a new candidate began to circulate. He was named as Leopold of Hohenzollern-Sigmaringen, a member of the junior, and Catholic, branch of the Prussian ruling house. The French Ambassador in Berlin, Benedetti, was instructed to check on these rumours, the Emperor informing him that: 'The candidature of the Prince of Hohenzollern is anti-national, the country will not put up with it and it must be prevented'. The feelings of the French Government were conveyed by Benedetti to Bismarck, who cannot have been displeased to find that this time he had drawn a winner. As a consequence, there was much to-ing and fro-ing between Madrid and Berlin during the autumn and winter of 1869–70, and on 15 March 1870 a Crown Council was held in Berlin to decide finally on the putting forward of the Hohenzollern candidature. This Council was ostensibly a 'family dinner', but since the guests of the King were Leopold and his father (Prince Anton), the Crown Prince of Prussia, Generals von Roon and von Moltke, plus Bismarck, it was certainly much more than that.

Six weeks later Leopold officially accepted the Spanish crown and the Spanish parliament announced its ratification of the acceptance on 1 July. By then Napoleon III, seriously alarmed by Bismarck's manoeuvres, had pushed for a simple solution which he hoped would satisfy all the interested parties and would block Bismarck. He had managed to persuade Isabella to abdicate formally, so that her young son could be proclaimed King and a Council of Regency established. This plan was deliberately sabotaged by an 'error' in a cyphered telegram, which gave the wrong date for the return of the Spanish envoy from Berlin to Madrid, making it seem that he would not return before 9 July. Since the Spanish parliament would adjourn from 1 July until November, there seemed to be no time to discuss alternatives and so, fearing the consequences of a hiatus, Leopold's acceptance was proclaimed by the Junta in Madrid [*Doc.* 22].

The news, which was received officially in Paris on 2 July, burst like a bomb. The newspapers, freed since 1868 from any censorship, adopted a highly bellicose tone which disturbed the government and alarmed the Emperor, who was fully aware of the seriousness of the crisis. Napoleon III did his best to dampen down the over-aggressive public reaction, but, as has been already indicated, the weakness of the ministry and the constitutional confusion made it difficult for him to operate successfully. The very shakiness of Ollivier's ministry made its members all the more determined to show a resolute attitude in the face of the 'Prussian threat' (as it was now called) in order to disarm its critics in the Chamber [74]. With this intention the Foreign Minister, the Duc de Gramont, speaking in the Legislative Body, made plain the government's resolve not to yield, and his statements were greeted enthusiastically by both government supporters and most of the opposition [11; 44].

The Emperor still attempted by his personal intervention to work for a peaceful solution, making it plain to the Spanish Ambassador that a simple withdrawal of the candidature would satisfy France. At the same time, however, he showed himself well aware of the deeper implications by saying: 'Do you think that M. de Bismarck, who has organised all this behind the scenes in order to provoke us, will let the occasion pass?'

European reaction was on the whole favourable to France, since most of the Powers saw how impossible it was that she should accept a Prussian candidate on the Spanish throne. This European reaction, together with intense diplomatic activity in Paris, led to the decision of Leopold to renounce the throne through the intermediary of his father. That France had gained a tremendous diplomatic victory was clear to all. Even Guizot, no friend to the regime, hailed it as 'the most splendid diplomatic triumph that I've seen in my whole life'. Unfortunately, it was to prove a hollow victory and war came on 19 July.

That it did come was in part due to the equivocal attitude of the King of Prussia when asked for guarantees that the candidature would not be renewed. It was also due in part to internal conditions in France. But the real culprit was Bismarck, whose Ems Telegram proved to be, as he hoped, 'the red rag to the Gallic bull'. He himself was to admit as much in later life [*Doc. 23*].

In the last resort, whatever the cause, France found herself committed to war against the foremost military power in Europe, and it was a war she was to fight alone. Italy would not move because the Italian Government hoped to profit from the situation by acquiring Rome. As for Austria-Hungary, she would not risk a second military confrontation with Prussia unless she was sure of France's success. The result was that, whatever can be said for or against Napoleon III's foreign policy, France was as isolated in Europe in 1870 as she had been in 1815. The consequences were to prove even more catastrophic.

DEFEAT AND DOWNFALL

French mobilisation revealed how poorly organised the army was; it was difficult to form regiments, difficult to get them to the front, and even more difficult to supply them adequately. A heavy price now had to be paid for the refusal to accept the Emperor's plans for military reform in 1867 [27]. The Emperor joined the army without any public ceremonies or rejoicing, and such manifestations as he encountered en route depressed rather than reassured him. As he remarked: 'Enthusiasm is a fine thing, but sometimes it is ridiculous'. He was convinced that the war would be difficult, and in his proclamation to his troops warned them that: 'You are going to fight one of the best armies in Europe'. The condition of his own army gave him little cause for satisfaction even before he arrived at his headquarters, where he found all in confusion. From the beginning the French suffered reverses, none of them decisive it is true, but all were grim indications of how the war might go. The immediate result of the initial failures was to bring about a political crisis in Paris, where the Empress-Regent had to accept the overthrow of Ollivier's Ministry on 9 August, and the constitution of a new one under General de Montauban, Comte de Palikao. Significantly, in view of future developments, the Empress was persuaded, by those who were already envisaging political changes, to constitute the new Ministry without any direct communication with the Emperor. He, on hearing the news, was astounded, but was unable to undo the damage. As for the new Ministry of Palikao, it could do nothing to affect the course of the war, now transformed into a full-scale Prussian invasion of France which the French armies seemed powerless to halt.

Convinced that the war was virtually lost, the conservative groups in Paris, fearing a revolutionary outbreak as much as military defeat, began to plan for some way of maintaining order. From their point of view, the important thing was to achieve some sort of legal transference of power which would prevent a hiatus in government, and would thus avoid giving any revolutionary group an opportunity to emerge. As early as 12 August *The Times* commented that: 'The dynasty which still reigns in France is commonly thought of as a thing of the past'. That, as far as the political cliques went, was the truth. The problem was that the dynasty still reigned and it was therefore essential to dislodge the Emperor. The Empress's lack of experience and the fact that after 10 August she was at the mercy of intrigues in Paris, meant that she could be discounted as a political force. She was, however, extremely important In a negative sense, since it was essential for the success of the planned transference of power that the Emperor be kept out of Paris. The Empress was therefore advised that any such return would be interpreted as cowardice and desertion of the army in face of the enemy. The result of this was that she refused to accept the idea even at a moment when the Emperor himself seemed inclined to think it was the correct move [44] [*Doc. 24*].

The political groups, led by Thiers, saw that having successfully eliminated the Empress-Regent as a factor in decision making, all that now remained to be done was to remove all vestige of power from Napoleon III. Already, on 12 August, he had abandoned command of the army to Marshal Bazaine: with his military power gone, the next step must be to reduce him to a political cypher. The man chosen for this task by the Paris politicians was General Trochu. A strong conservative, Catholic and royalist in his political convictions, Trochu seemed the ideal candidate for a transfer of power without fuss, not least because he shared the apprehensions of the politicians about the possibility of a revolutionary outbreak in Paris. The plan was that Trochu should go to the front and persuade the Emperor to name him military governor of Paris. This would have the double advantage of giving the General full military *and*, in the case of an emergency, civil powers in the city. The Emperor, reluctant to abandon all semblance of authority, agreed to the scheme only because Trochu made it plain that he was seeking a purely temporary authority in order to prepare for Napoleon III's return to the capital. Since it was already known that the Empress would fiercely oppose any move by the Emperor to return to Paris, Trochu was certainly guilty of deceit, if not of treason.

Things fell out as planned. The Empress did urge the Emperor not to return, while at the same time Trochu was able to install himself in Paris as military governor by the Emperor's authority. He was thus in charge at the critical moment of 3/4 September, when news arrived of the Emperor's surrender with his army at Sedan.

4   THE PROVISIONAL GOVERNMENT

Although the political cliques in Paris had expected a military defeat, they had not anticipated the swiftness and totality of the disaster which occurred at Sedan, and so there was a moment of confusion when no one seemed able to produce a political response. The deputies in the Legislative Body, who could perhaps have salvaged something of the regime had they had sufficient courage and resolution, failed totally to respond to the moment. Together with Trochu, they abandoned the Empress, who was forced to flee, while the conservative groups, hoping to prevent radical excesses, left it to the Republican opposition to cope with a situation which they had not foreseen or wished. Any hesitancy the Republican leaders may have felt was overcome by the beginnings of a popular insurrection in Paris, which awakened all their fears of a revolution, so they took the lead in proclaiming the Republic with the maximum of drama and the minimum of disturbance. That they were able to achieve a revolution without bloodshed was due largely to the fact that Trochu, who cooperated with them, had the military forces in Paris under his control. So the revolution had, after all, been avoided and the transfer of power had been peacefully accomplished. As Jules Ferry, one of the Republican leaders, said: 'It was a carnival; never was a revolution carried out with such gentleness' [47].

The new Provisional Government in Paris, with Trochu at its head, was composed largely of the leading Republican deputies who had formed the opposition group in the Chamber during the Empire. Since none of them had 'revolutionary' antecedents, it was fairly safe to assume that the cause of conservatism had triumphed and that politics could resume their normal course. In fact it was not so simple. There was the war to be dealt with and that posed serious problems; not just the obvious military ones, but the less obvious, though equally important, political ones. Here the Republicans were unfortunate, for they were associated in the popular mind with the idea of a general call to arms for the defence of the country. This was in part the consequence of their claim to the inheritance of the Revolutionary Wars of 1792–3, and in part due to their own political statements in more recent years. It will be recalled that their opposition in 1867 to the Emperor's army reforms had been based on the idea of a general mobilisation of the population as the answer to an invasion of the Motherland. Indeed, during the last days of August 1870 they had made speeches in the Chamber demanding the arming of the nation. These chickens now came home to roost and it was confidently expected that the new Republican Ministers would decree such a mobilisation, arm the populace, and drive the invaders out of France in no time at all [*Doc. 25*].

THE REPUBLICAN WAR, SEPTEMBER 1870–MARCH 1871

After 4 September the Republican leaders found themselves faced with the realities which come with actual responsibility. They knew perfectly well that the 'nation in arms' was unrealisable and dangerous nonsense and they were also fully convinced that the war was lost. Above all, they were not overanxious to arm the populace, in particular that of Paris. However, victims of their own rhetoric, they were aware that if they did *not* prosecute the war they ran the risk of being overthrown by a *real* revolutionary movement, and all their attempts to avoid an upheaval would have been rendered useless. In these circumstances they attempted to do two things simultaneously; they announced that the war would go on – but also made it clear that it would only be fought by properly constituted armies of the Republic. Distribution of arms, other than to the military, would be confined to citizens who enrolled in the National Guard as an authorised militia force. These measures would, it was hoped, prevent the indiscriminate arming of those who could well prove a danger to lawfully established authority, while at the same time removing the charges of half-heartedness in the prosecution of the war which were already being made against them [23].

Parallel with its publicly declared intention of carrying on the war, the Provisional Government secretly sought to make peace with the Germans, who since 20 September had encircled Paris with their armies. On that same day Jules Favre, one of the Republican Ministers, had contacted Bismarck to sound him out on possible peace terms. When news of this leaked out in Paris, there was an outburst of anger in the streets at this revelation of governmental duplicity which forced Favre into making a proclamation containing the phrase: 'The enemy shall not take from us an inch of our territory nor a stone of our fortresses'. This claptrap merely gave unnecessary hostages to fortune and was to rebound savagely on the heads of the members of the government in 1871 when peace finally had to be made.

Furthermore, because of the revelations of 20 September the extreme revolutionary groups remained suspicious of ministerial activity and henceforward scented treason in what was simply military weakness. An unfortunate combination of circumstances tended to reinforce this popular view when, on 31 October, a severe defeat of the French at Bourget on the outskirts of Paris coincided with the news of Bazaine's surrender of the last intact French army at Metz, where he had been besieged. When it was discovered that at the same time Thiers was once again trying for an armistice with the Prussians, the long-dreaded insurrection erupted in Paris. Many of the Ministers were seized and an attempt was made to proclaim a 'Committee of Public Safety' and a 'Revolutionary Commune', which institutions, it was felt, would be enough in themselves to frighten the Prussians. They certainly frightened the ministers, who were only saved by the intervention of loyal troops led by Trochu, who suppressed the revolutionary organisations before they had time to establish themselves, thus precariously restoring political order.

THE REPUBLICAN PEACE, MARCH 1871

The Germans now began the siege of Paris in earnest, and although the war continued sporadically in other parts of France, it was becoming clear to most responsible people that the situation had to be ended, since victory over Germany was virtually impossible. This point of view was particularly prevalent in the countryside, where the prolongation of hostilities exacerbated the Prussians and led to increasing brutality on the part of the soldiers, from which the peasantry suffered most. Convinced that the time for action was long overdue, Favre, on 28 January, signed an armistice with the German high command. It was, quite simply, a capitulation.

With the war's end, the government of National Defence felt it essential to hold elections in order to have a legitimately constituted National Assembly which could authorise a formal peace. The elections revealed a division between rural and urban France, in that the countryside *en bloc* returned conservative deputies, most of them monarchist, while the towns returned Republicans. The pattern of the last elections held under the Empire was repeated, though in view of the discrediting of the former regime it is not surprising that only twenty Bonapartist deputies were returned. In the popular mind the Republicans were associated with a desire to continue the war, while the conservatives stood for peace, and the issue of the election could not be in doubt. As a reminder of what was at stake, the voters needed only to note that 43 Departments of France were occupied by the enemy. No wonder that the peasantry had, *en masse*, voted for peace, irrespective of the political colour of the candidate [23; 25].

In mid-February the new government established itself at Bordeaux, on the grounds that neither Paris nor Versailles was suitable because of the presence of the German armies. In Paris, where the news of the monarchist complexion of the Assembly had resulted in an outburst of fury, the decision to set up the government outside the capital was seen as another grievance. When news arrived on 15 March that the preliminaries of peace had been ratified, and that the terms included a huge indemnity plus the loss of Alsace-Lorraine, Paris moved from anger to revolt. The government, led by Thiers as 'Head of the Executive Power' (for no one was anxious to establish a formal Presidency), had by now moved from Bordeaux in order to establish itself at Versailles, thereby depriving Paris of its 'normal' position as capital. It was this second slight which finally encouraged the more radical members of the political groups within the city to proclaim the Commune, thus formally putting Paris outside the jurisdiction of a government which seemed not to want to return there.

5 THE COMMUNE OF PARIS, MARCH–MAY 1871

It has been argued that Thiers and his ministers deliberately provoked the Commune in order to be able to teach Paris a lesson when the time came to call it to order, and that this was why the Assembly set itself up at Versailles. As evidence for this view, the government's decision to disarm the National Guard and other groups is held to have been an act of provocation, calculated to bring about a confrontation with the city. On the other hand, it must be said that the government's decision was based on the fact that the Communards claimed to have 300,000 men under arms, including cannon and machine guns, and it is difficult to see how any legal authority could allow such a body to exist in what were now peacetime conditions. However, the fact that Thiers was fiercely conservative, would have liked to suppress universal suffrage, and hated what he called 'the vile rabble', made it easy to make the charge of deliberate provocation stick. Nevertheless, there is no direct evidence that anything other than irritation with the action of the Parisians and a desire to restore normal government lay behind his decisions [23; 48].

The Commune itself has, as an historical episode, become so overlaid with myths originating on the left and the right of the political spectrum that it is difficult to disentangle fact from fiction. Whatever subsequent conclusions have been drawn from the episode by protagonists of either left-wing or right-wing views, it must be remembered that at the time it was a specific response to a particular situation. Conditions within Paris, more than any ideological programme, created the circumstances which made the Commune possible. In this context it is significant that attempts to found 'sister communes' in the cities of Lyons and Marseilles failed totally.

It will be recalled that an attempt had already been made to establish a revolutionary commune during the outbreak of October 1870, with a view to thwarting the suspected peace projects of the government and forcing it to prosecute the war more vigorously. Although in March 1871 this attitude seemed irrelevant, since the war was already over, there is no doubt that a spirit of bellicosity still dominated many of the Communards. Indeed, some of the more radical members of the Commune wanted to mount an attack on the government in Versailles as a sort of substitute for the war. To some extent the whole affair of the Commune has the air of a bizarre historical pageant whose participants attempted to reenact the 'great days' of the Revolution of 1792–3. The leadership in 1871 made constant references to what had happened during those years to the enemies of the Republic. Whether these enemies were at home, in the shape of aristocrats and counter-revolutionaries, or had come in the shape of foreign armies, their intentions had been thwarted only by the actions of revolutionary Paris. To such men, the government of September, and even more so the new government of Thiers, were traitors and by inference, counter-revolutionary. They had made peace with the enemy and they had accepted the dismemberment of the Republic, which, by historical definition, was 'One and Indivisible'.

While this historicism was one of the strands, and a very important one, making up the fabric of the Communards' thinking, a more up-to-date note was struck by the attitude of a minority. This smaller fraction saw in the Commune an expression of the aspirations of the Socialist International and they rejected, for the most part, the Jacobin traditions of 1792–3, with their emphasis on central direction and ultrapatriotism. According to the minority view, the Commune should represent the first step in the dismantling of the centralised state dating from the Revolution and Napoleon I, with a view to replacing it by a federated group of autonomous Communes. In addition to this administrative reorientation, the minority demanded that the Republic be egalitarian and socialist, as well as democratic [23].

Although this more radical faction succeeded in achieving some of its aims in the period from March to May, it never really captured control of the Commune. Its triumph was posthumous, in that later adherents to the left-wing interpretation of 1871 saw in the Commune a proletarian uprising and the harbinger of a new era of social, as opposed to political, revolution. Considerable substance was given to this view by the brutal and savagely repressive actions of the conservative, rightist government which accompanied the ending of the Commune. After all, if the Commune had not been a real socialist rising, why were the possessing classes so terrified by it?

In fact, the Commune was never 'socialist' in a revolutionary sense, and certainly it was never Marxist. Through the months of its existence, controlling power remained in the hands of 'respectable' Republican radicals, and this was all the more extraordinary since the electoral process was extremely democratic. Given that direct election was the norm, and also that those who were elected were at all times responsible to their electors, who could remove them if they failed to act properly as their representatives, it could reasonably be assumed that the electors would choose radical and progressive candidates. Yet an analysis of the 90 elected to the Central Committee, which was the nearest thing to a governing body the Commune had, shows that there were only 35 workers, the rest being made up of doctors, lawyers, etc. One historian of the Commune has provided us with an interesting breakdown of this directing body:

> The Council finally consisted of eighty-one members, though Cluseret (military co-ordinator) seldom had time to attend and many others absented themselves with far less justification. ... A good attendance was around sixty. ... About eighteen members came from middle-class backgrounds from which they had broken away during their school and student days. ... In all there were about thirty members of the Commune who could be classed as from the professions, belonging to *la bohème*, in many cases a term of abuse at the time, half of whom had been journalists on Republican papers. The others included three doctors, and a vet ... three lawyers and three members of the teaching profession. ... Eleven were in commerce or worked as clerks. ... Thirty-five on the Commune were manual workers or had been before becoming involved in revolutionary politics. ... These were mainly craftsmen in the small workshops that made up the long-established trades of the capital. Typical of this group were copper, bronze and other metal workers, carpenters, masons, house decorators ... [23 pp. 204–5].

As for the Socialist International, it succeeded in obtaining only four seats, a number which reflected its minority position within the Commune as a whole. Even more striking is the fact that of the 90 delegates elected, 16 refused to serve because they rejected the breach with the government at Versailles. In the subsequent by-elections held in April to replace them, the voting was so low that many candidates did not receive enough votes to be elected. Popular enthusiasm had quickly dissipated as the gravity of the initial action began to be understood and fear of the consequences began to be felt. Far from being a homogeneous, revolutionary, proletarian body, as the Left would have it, or a group of highly organised International revolutionary socialists, as the Right claimed, the Commune was a heterogeneous group, seriously divided as to its aims and purpose [23]. This is, of course, totally comprehensible if it is borne in mind that the Commune was not a planned but a spontaneous event, and that few of its leading participants had any clearly formulated political ideas. In a sense they knew what they did not want, but had no elaborate theories of state organisation to replace what they hoped to overthrow. It was this absence of political formulae which explains the historical, and backward-looking, nature of such political ideas as were current.

In matters of social legislation, the Communards showed themselves to be in the mainstream of progressive ideas circulating in France at the time – insofar as they could be applied to Paris. They were interested in promoting education, in regulating hours of work and in trying to improve the social status of women. But in a sense these policies were not new, they were merely an extension of existing social trends which had been prevalent during the Empire and which had been reflected in the attitudes of both government and its critics. Much more revealing, in assessing the extent of revolutionary socialism within the Commune, is the fact that throughout the entire period the gold reserve of the Bank of France went untouched and that the Bank actually advanced money to the Commune. Neither side wished to see the collapse of credit in the value of paper money, which would almost certainly have happened had the Bank's assets been 'socialised'.

When it came to private property, the Commune showed itself scrupulously legalistic in its approach; only abandoned workshops might be taken over by groups of workers who hoped to set up cooperative workshops on the premises, and the original owners were promised compensation for their seized premises when they returned. In all the moves which were made on behalf of the workers the stress was on the co-operative aspect, or quite simply one of social assistance. One such move was the setting up of the Labour and Exchange Commission which the workers had hoped for because it actually had relevance to their living and working conditions. Its stated aim was: 'To propagate social doctrines; find ways of equalising labour and the wages paid to it', but it hardly got further than the stage of this declaration of good intentions, though it did help in the organisation of unions and workers' associations.

The Commune was, of course, attempting to operate in Paris not only in the sphere of social policies, but also in the daily struggle to feed the populace and to maintain essential services such as gas, water and sewage. It had to do all of these things while at the same time keeping a watchful eye on what the government at Versailles might be planning. Both sides knew that sooner or later there would have to be an armed attack, in order to end the situation one way or another – and the Communards confidently expected Thiers to move in on the city.

At Versailles, the government was willing but unable to do just what the Communards feared. Thiers found that the only troops he had to hand were so demoralised by the defeats and the events of 1870–71 as to be little more than a drunken and disorderly rabble. There was a shortage of officers and senior non-commissioned officers, many of whom were prisoners in Germany and were not released until March 1871, after the signing of the Treaty ending the war. It was the necessity to reconstruct a sound and disciplined army, which could be relied upon to fight, which prevented Thiers from taking military action much sooner than he did [48].

Of paramount importance in the calculations of the Versailles government was the fact that the army was going to fight against *Frenchmen*. In a civil war, that most cruel and fearful of all wars, it is essential that the army be prepared psychologically as well as militarily to fire upon its fellow countrymen. For that reason the government represented the Communards as dominated by foreign adventurers, a sort of international riff-raff, whose actions were simply another insult and injury to a country already martyred by the events of the recent war. Even those who were French by birth and residence were designated as the lowest of the social classes, criminals, ex-convicts and layabouts, only interested in plunder, rape and murder. 'They steal public funds and savings ... they loot private houses ...' – such was the refrain of government propaganda. To make a sharper point for the soldiers of rural origin, it was announced that the Communards intended to force the provinces to feed Paris for nothing, so that they could live without working. Above all, capital was made of the fact that thanks to the Commune, the Prussian army could enjoy the spectacle of Frenchmen killing one another, while the press in Germany was able to make much of the 'rottenness' of France.

Little by little, discipline combined with incessant propaganda to make the army reliable enough to be used against Paris, though there remained many soldiers who sympathised with aspects of the

Commune and who, coming from different social strata, tended not to look at events from the same standpoint as their officers. Nevertheless, by May it was felt that an offensive against the city could be launched, since a sufficient number of troops could be relied on to do their duty. After preliminary fighting, the city was entered on 21 May [23; 48].

Even before the launching of the government's offensive, in fact from the first week in May, the Commune had been breaking down as an organised entity. All the political difficulties and differences, never resolved, now took their toll in the form of the abandoning of posts of responsibility. Central direction ceased, there was no overall military plan to defend the city against the Versaillais, and the battles were based on local responses to the general threat. Barricades had been erected to provide a means of defence, but if some were massive constructions needing artillery to demolish them, others were haphazard collections of furniture, paving stones, boxes, etc., which were not strong enough to withstand assault by regular troops. Another basic weakness of the Commune was revealed in that men refused to leave their own *quartiers* to go to the help of other hard-pressed areas. This parochialism had been a marked feature of the Commune from its inception, but what had been merely irritating as a political manifestation proved fatal in the context of defending the city. In fairness, it must be said that even a coordinated defence would probably have been of little use once the army was launched into a full-scale battle. Wordy proclamations were no substitute for military efficiency [*Doc. 26*].

From 21 May to 28 May Paris endured what has been called *la semaine sanglante* (the bloody week) in which both sides engaged in the conflict committed fearful atrocities. Many were committed in the heat of battle; too many more were the result of premeditation. The army must be held responsible for actually carrying out the reprisals against the Communards or, as one writer puts it: '*La semaine sanglante* was the work of the generals'. Nevertheless, the moral and political authority behind their brutality came from the government, which means that Thiers must himself bear much of the burden of responsibility. Not that the atrocities were all one-sided. In that respect the Communards gave as good as they got. They had taken hostages who included many priests (the Archbishop of Paris among them) and others whom they considered to be representatives of an oppressive religious and social structure. These were now despatched in circumstances so tenuously legal as to make their executions simply murder in cold blood [48].

By the middle of the week large areas of central Paris were in flames, partly as the result of shelling, and partly of deliberate arson, as the Communards' more violent souls attempted to 'take Paris with them'. Most of the major public buildings of Paris, including the Tuileries Palace and the Hôtel de Ville, were destroyed, as well as whole streets, for the fires soon got out of control since there was no water even when the fire brigades did appear.

The last two days produced scenes of horror which were to be remembered later with pride, or disgust, depending on the political viewpoint. Everyone had reasons for justifying or execrating what took place, as if the whole thing were not the triumph of madness rather than reason. No one has ever agreed on a final total of the number of Parisians dead as a result of that week, but a figure of 20,000 is hardly an exaggerated one. On the army side the figure seems to be 877 dead and some 6,800 wounded. More than 38,000 prisoners were taken by government forces, of whom over 20,000 were sent to forced labour within France, while over 5,000 were deported to New Caledonia. Many others were sent to penal battalions in Algeria. It all added up to a fearful accounting, and the spectacle of the total suspension of law, justice and humanity in the city which had been the pride of France and the envy of Europe, was not an edifying one. The fact that the city itself lay half in ruins was a terrible tribute to the ferocity of the destructive impulse which had run parallel with the urge to kill. It was a jolt to the optimistic belief that the nineteenth century was one of upward progress, and the effect upon the 'possessing classes' of European society was to increase their terror of revolution [23; 78; 82].

Contrariwise, the more the right-wing and conservatives spoke of the Commune as the harbinger of red revolution, which only timely and resolute intervention had stifled, the more the left-wing ideology profited from it. What had been in essence an unplanned, sporadic action became transmuted by a flood of publications into a glorious step along the road to the ultimate triumph of the proletariat [*Doc. 27*].

So much historical myth has accumulated around the events of March–May 1871 that it requires an effort of will to look beyond and through the accretions. Yet, as one scholar has pointed out: '... it is possible to see Paris naked, for its conventional clothes were suddenly removed', and since the Commune was in and of Paris, it might perhaps be well to consider the city itself as one of the main protagonists. Some of the Communards were themselves conscious of how Parisian the business was. Vallès, a writer and journalist who held office under the Commune, wrote: 'We are all marching under the same banner, the spirit of Paris'. And again, hailing the city as a living entity: 'Oh splendid Paris! What cowards we were when we talked of abandoning you and your districts which we thought were dead! Forgive us, fatherland of honour, city of salvation, encampment of the Revolution'. This sense of 'Parisness' runs through much of the rhetoric both during and after the events of March to May, and it indicates a special symbiotic relationship between the Communards and the city.

Since the nineteenth century was, *par excellence*, the century of urban growth, contemporaries found themselves fascinated by the process of urbanisation, not least because of its possible political implications. The historical importance of the city, as contributing to the growth, or decline, of states, became an object of interest to scholars. In 1864 Fustel de Coulanges, one of the leading French historians of the day, published *La cité antique*, a work of enormous importance, in which Coulanges stressed the role of the city in determining the development of societies in the Ancient World. His assertions not only reflected the contemporary interest in urbanism, but provided a further stimulus to discussion by those who saw the city as a key to the development of their own world. The revolutionary outbreaks of 1830, and even more those of 1848, were seen essentially as urban phenomena, which in many instances had owed their impetus to the breakdown of old municipal and social structures. Cities like Vienna, Berlin, and Paris, all centres of revolution in 1848, had all suffered sharp and sudden expansions of population for which the authorities were ill-prepared, and which had led to a virtual breakdown of even semi-decent living for large numbers of the inhabitants.

In Paris, the experience of 1848, together with the social plans of Napoleon III, led to a substantial rebuilding of large areas of the city between 1850 and 1870, carried out by Haussmann, Prefect of the Seine, with the direct encouragement and support of the Emperor. Between them, they had produced a city which was both modern and beautiful, and certainly a great deal healthier than the one that had existed in 1848. The construction of elaborate sewage systems, plus the provision of water which was no longer almost poisonous, had done much to eradicate the worst diseases and epidemics, such as cholera, which had occurred sporadically from 1830 to 1848. Paris was lighter, more airy, cleaner and better organised than it had ever been in its existence. Attempts had even been made to provide better housing for the workers by the building of various *Cités Napoléon*, a form of municipal housing, which provided reasonable accommodation at low rents. In addition to this, the opening up of large open spaces in both the wealthier and the poorer districts made the city a place of relaxation as well as work [55; 69].

Nevertheless, life in Paris remained hard for the bulk of the population, however much conditions improved, and as the wealth of the city increased, as it did during the Empire, the gulf between rich and poor was accentuated. Not only that, the rebuilding programme, which had brought about the demolition of what we would now call areas of inner-city neglect, and the construction of new, but more expensive apartment buildings, pushed the poorer groups out of the centre. More and more, 'Monumental Paris' dominated the centre – the great Boulevards, the new Palace of Justice, the Louvre-Tuileries agglomeration – while the suburbs housed the mass of the population. To many of these people the city became an object of hatred since it appeared to them that, pitilessly, it crushed or exploited them. In this seemingly soulless and callous environment those who struggled to maintain themselves, either clinging desperately to honesty, or by taking to crime, could not but feel a desire for revenge. Attempts by the government to build housing estates, the *Cités Napoléon*, to provide homes for workers and the lower paid together with regulations controlling the price of bread could only be palliatives, while private charity was regarded as insulting. The city, it seemed, did not care; nor did those who ran it, whether government or magistrates. Is it any wonder that in the last days of the Commune great public buildings should have been singled out for destruction?

The nature of the city's population had much to do with this sense of injustice and resentment, in that among the settled citizens there were many of the unstable elements found in all metropolitan areas; new immigrants who had come in from the country (the population rose by 650,000 in 1850–71) and who found it hard to adjust to city life, or even to find work. Once freed from the normal constraints of the police, as happened during the Commune, these groups were seldom held back by considerations of what their neighbours might think, or what they might lose in an upheaval. They had no settled neighbours and all too often they had nothing to lose. For them, the end of orderly, routine life was a chance to break out and to feel that by associating themselves with the Commune they had become truly Parisian and had found an identity.

The revolutionary tradition, rooted in the city's recent history, had been given a new impetus since 1869, when freedom of the press and the right of public meeting had led to an upsurge in the number of political clubs and societies; but a noteworthy feature of this movement had been its traditional, radical and anti-clerical basis. Given that the Parisian working population was artisanal rather than proletarian, this was hardly surprising, and indeed it explains many of the politico-social attitudes of the Communards. Precisely because the pattern of revolution was traditional and artisanal, many of the other groups felt alienated, and it was not accidental that the more militant and violent of the Communards came from the 'newer' areas of the city like Clichy-Batignolles. The traditional revolutionary areas, the Faubourgs of Saint Antoine and Saint Marcel, kept to the straight, traditional Republican line, even if their representatives expressed it in fairly sharp and radical terms [23].

Marx had warned that: 'French workmen ... must not allow themselves to be deluded by the national memories of 1792. ... They have not to recapitulate the past, but to build up the future'. Those in Paris in 1871 ignored Marx's warning, partly because they were not sure of the future they wanted to build, but also because they felt they would have betrayed the city which had been the cradle of revolution since 1789. Interestingly enough, it was for much the same reason that the government was determined to crush the Commune, and it helps to explain the fearful repression of the *semaine sanglante*. The mythology of the 'evil city' was equally potent in its action on both Left and Right, though for different reasons. To talk of the Commune of Paris without actually talking about Paris is, therefore, to miss a point which contemporaries certainly saw. The location of the event was no accident.

The year 1870–71 is known in France as the terrible year. The defeat, the fall of the Empire, the Commune, the loss of Alsace-Lorraine, and the general breakdown, albeit temporary, of the norms of society, were to leave a scar on French life which has possibly not yet healed. The years between 1848 and 1870 had seemed, in spite of all the defects of the Imperial system, years of stability, economic and social progress, and, at the end, peaceful political evolution. The events of one year showed how fragile it all was. France had once again to rebuild and to find a new political and social order. The Republic was chosen to represent the form of the State, but it was a form which took a long time to acquire a substance. One of the bitter political gibes made during the first decades of its existence was: 'How splendid the Republic was – under the Empire'.

PART THREE: ASSESSMENT

Any attempt to assess the historical significance of the Second Empire must begin with a reminder of the conditions in which Louis Napoleon/Napoleon III emerged as leader. The breakdown of the political order which characterised the end of the reign of Louis-Philippe was the recognition that the government framework no longer functioned in the interests of society in general. At the same time, the political stalemate established by Guizot and the King, lampooned as 'the principle of Chinese immobility', was paralleled by an equally timid approach to economic and social problems. The revolution of 1848 came therefore at a particularly dangerous moment, when lack of political direction coincided with a great deal of social unrest. Fortunately for the ruling elite, the social unrest was originally unfocused and when the discontented sought a focus for their aspirations they found it in the person of Louis Napoleon Bonaparte, who had for different reasons become the choice of the 'men of order'. So Louis Napoleon provided an apparent link between the masses on the one hand, and sectional or class interests on the other. Through the action of universal suffrage, the masses elected him while the classes accepted him.

There was, however, one significant difference between the two groups in their attitude to the regime. The masses remained loyal, while the large majority of the classes ranged in their attitude from lukewarm support to scarcely veiled hostility. This hostility remained quiescent during the first decade of the Empire when sectional interest was subordinate to an economic growth which involved a massive transformation of French society. Freed from the debilitating effects of party struggle which had characterised the period from 1815 to 1848, the Emperor's plan to bring about social change by means of economic growth made great progress. The will, and the ability, to use new financial policies, coupled with the transport revolution, did produce a society in which all groups benefited, even if not equally.

Unfortunately, the regime was obliged to rely for much of its political force on those who were not wholly committed to it. While not necessarily seeking its downfall, they hoped at least to gain control in order to reshape it in their own interests. 'Orthodox' finance and protectionist economics, rejecting the ideas of Saint-Simonianism, combined with a dislike of imperial foreign policy to produce from the 1860s an increasing hostility to Napoleon III's policies. The resurgence of the political groups produced an attempt by the Emperor to come to terms with them, while retaining overall direction and leadership. But the contradictions involved in doing this – that is, how to produce a 'liberal' Empire while avoiding a parliamentary monarchy – proved extremely difficult. This is not to say that the Empire would not have overcome its difficulties. The plebiscite of May 1870 revealed a degree of mass support which was a comfort to Napoleon III and a grave disappointment to his opponents. In any event, it has to be remembered that whatever the future held was never to be discovered, because the regime foundered in September 1870.

Nevertheless, the force which destroyed the Empire was an external and not an internal one. Had Napoleon III's foreign policy been more successful, or to put it another way, had other European powers seen more clearly what was at stake, France might have been supported and Bismarck thwarted. But the 'ifs' of history form no basis for real analysis. France *was* alone, and the regime *did* founder. As for Napoleon III, he spent the period from September 1870 to March 1871 in captivity in Germany, unable to influence the subsequent course of events. Refusing to deal with Bismarck, he also refused to accept the new regime in France which he claimed had neither legality nor popular sanction (i.e. plebiscite) to justify it.

In March 1871 he came to England and settled at Chislehurst, where the Empress and the Prince Imperial were already established. Although he maintained links with former ministers such as Rouher and Ollivier, he had little direct influence, except as a rallying point for survivors of the Empire. His own health, which had been precarious since the mid-Sixties, deteriorated sharply, and by the winter of 1872 it was clear that only surgery could provide any hope of relief. The Emperor suffered from stones in the kidney, a disease both crippling in its effects, because of the severe pain it caused, and dangerous in its treatment, since the operation was extremely perilous. Although at first the surgeons hoped for a successful outcome, the Emperor succumbed to general weakness and infection. He died on 9 January 1873.

What had Napoleon III achieved? Had his Empire been no more

than an interval in the evolution of modern France? Historians hostile to both the man and his politics answered that he achieved nothing, and that his Empire was brutal, repressive and a sham imitation of that of his uncle. The progress of historical research and, in the case of French historians, a cooling of political passions, have led to an abandonment of this intransigent position. Nowadays, there are many historians willing to admit that Napoleon III was an idealist who did sincerely believe in his attempts to bring about social justice and improve the lot of the masses. They also see the Empire as a period of economic prosperity which brought real and lasting benefits to France. Often, however, these same historians attack the political aspects of the regime, condemning Napoleon III for incapacity where they do not accuse him of brutality and repression.

A smaller group of historians have attempted to see Napoleon III as someone who was indeed motivated by a sincere desire to improve social and economic conditions, which he did achieve. This historical view holds that the structure of French political life, and the personnel who were engaged in running it, made political *and* social progress extremely difficult for Napoleon III by thwarting him at various levels of government. In this context it is significant that although the Emperor never attempted to justify himself when, after 1870, he was subjected to a campaign of vilification and calumny, he did occasionally react against those who accused him of never having done anything for the masses of the people.

The achievements were not insignificant. Apart from the general raising of the level of prosperity, in itself leading to an amelioration of life for the bulk of the population, there were the specific benefits of social legislation: relief for old age, the mutual aid societies, the maintenance of low bread prices by the *caisse de la boulangerie*, the provision of hospitals and convalescent homes for injured workers. While all of these measures can be dismissed as mere paternalistic palliatives, those who derived benefit from them may have been less critical. Certainly the legalising of the right to strike and the freedom of public meeting were of enormous and indisputable benefit to the workers, while the Emperor's patronage of the Workers' International showed where his inclinations lay – even if he could not always follow them.

At a political level, twenty years' experience of universal suffrage had made it impossible to revert to a restricted franchise. In 1871 Thiers and his fellow ministers would have liked to reduce the franchise, so that they could manipulate a smaller electorate, but they were afraid of the consequences of manifesting too openly this reactionary intent. They did manage to do away with the plebiscite as a means of popular sanction by denouncing it as a 'Bonapartist-caesarean device'. By this means any popular sanction of the executive, that is the president, was prevented. Only with the advent of the Fifth Republic in 1958 and the Presidency of General de Gaulle was the principle of direct election of the head of state reintroduced (1962). Significantly, this was done by means of a plebiscite – another echo from the period of the Empire. Little wonder that critics of the Fifth Republic see it as an expression of a 'moribund Bonapartism'. The shade of Napoleon III may well be amused.

Some historians have argued that the Second Empire represented a hiatus in the development of modern France. The regime is seen as being a time of repression, reaction and stagnation. In reality the Third Republic, with its feeble governments, its political conservatism and its hesitant economic growth, seems a better candidate for this sort of criticism. The events of 1940–45 served brutally to awaken the country from a kind of political and economic torpor, particularly the latter.

At the end of the Second World War there was a resurgence of Saint-Simonianism, as exemplified in the Monnet Plan with its emphasis on economic growth monitored by the state, and based on the concept of economic prosperity leading to political harmony. Ultimately this was to influence the course of events leading to the setting up of the European Economic Community. It is possible to see the Second Empire of Napoleon III as not so remote a precursor of these achievements.

PART FOUR: DOCUMENTS

DOCUMENT 1 LOUIS NAPOLEON STATES HIS CASE

In truth, if my government has not been able to carry through all the improvements which it envisaged, the fault lies with the manoeuvres of those factions which paralyse the goodwill of assemblies as well as that of governments who are devoted to the public good. For three years, you will have noticed that I have always been supported when it is a question of dealing with disorder by means of methods of suppression. But when I wanted to do something worthwhile, found the *Crédit Foncier*, take steps to improve the lot of the mass of the people, I have met with total apathy. ... A new phase in our political life is beginning. From one end of France to the other petitions are being signed demanding a revision of the Constitution. I await with confidence the expression of public opinion and the decision of the Assembly, which can only be inspired by a consideration of public good. If France makes it plain that no one has the right to dispose of her without her consent, France has only to say so: my courage and my energy will not be found wanting.

Since I have been in power I have shown how much I was indifferent to things which touched me personally since the public good was not at issue. The most unjust and violent attacks have been unable to move me. Whatever duties the country imposes on me it will find me ready to follow its will, and believe me, Gentlemen, France will not founder in my hands.

Louis Napoleon Bonaparte [10] Vol. 3, p. 211 Dijon, June 1851.

DOCUMENT 2 PLANS TO OVERTHROW THE PRESIDENT

It was known that on the day that the proposition of the Questeurs [to take control of the army away from the President] was rejected, it had been adopted that the president should be *décrété d'accusation* [accused of conspiracy against the state] and sent to the prison of Vincennes; and besides that there was a conspiracy in favour of the Prince de Joinville [a son of Louis Philippe] which only wanted an opportunity to break out.

Kerry, Earl of, (ed.) *The Secret of the Coup d'Etat*, Constable, London 1924, p. 127.

DOCUMENT 3   THE FAILURE OF THE REPUBLICANS TO
ALLY WITH LOUIS NAPOLEON

All the misfortunes of the Mountain [the Republicans] come from its failure
to embrace resolutely the opportunity which had been created; [that is] to
accept for what it was its temporary alliance with the Elysée and to follow
its consequences through to the end. But over-excited passions and deeply
felt resentments left no place for such considerations. Instead of adopting a
totally personal opposition to Louis Napoleon it had only to keep quiet and
share the fruits of his victory.

Pierre Joseph Proudhon, *Napoléon III* (ed. Clément Rochel), Société
d'éditions littéraires et artistiques, Paris, 1900, p.243.

DOCUMENT 4   THE *COUP D'ÉTAT* JUSTIFIED BY LOUIS
NAPOLEON

Proclamation of the President of the Republic, 2 December 1851.
Frenchmen! The present situation can no longer continue. Each day that
passes increases the country's dangers. The Assembly, which should be a
bastion of order, has become a centre for conspiracies. The patriotism of
three hundred of its members has not been able to stop these fatal
tendencies. Instead of making laws in the general interest, it is forging arms
for a civil war; it is encroaching on the authority which I hold directly from
the people; it encourages everv unhealthy discontent; it compromises the
tranquillity of France. I have dissolved it, and I make the people supreme
judge between it and me. The Constitution, as you know, had been drawn
up with a view to weakening, from the start, the power which you had
given me. Six million votes were a striking protest against it. Nevertheless, I
obeyed it faithfully. But now that the fundamental pact is no longer
respected by the same people who unceasingly invoke it, and that the men
who have already brought down two monarchies want to tie my hands, in
order to overthrow the Republic, my duty is to thwart their treacherous
schemes, to maintain the Republic and to save the country by invoking the
solemn judgement of the only sovereign I recognise in France, the People.

L.N. Bonaparte [10], Vol. 3, pp. 271-2.

DOCUMENT 5 CONSERVATIVE OPPOSITION TO SOCIAL
REFORMS

*The Council [of State] continually opposed those projects of the Emperor
which it considered badly thought out, Utopian, and vaguely socialist.*

In the Council of State Napoleon III was considered to be totally Utopian.
Every time a project bearing the imprint of the Emperor's personal cabinet
turned up, it was shuffled around, cut up, and emasculated in such a way
that it was firmly destined to be abortive.

V. Wright [50], p. 83.

DOCUMENT 6 LAW OF 25 MAY 1864 ON WORKERS'
COALITIONS

*Because of the difficulty of manoeuvring a progressive law through the
conservative Legislative Body, its supporters were compelled to adopt a
subterfuge. By disallowing violent strikes, they contrived to make peaceful
ones legal.*

Whoever leads or maintains, attempts to lead or maintain, an organised
stoppage of work, with the aim of forcing wages to be raised or lowered, or
to interfere with the free practice of industry or work, by means of duress,
assault, menaces, or fraudulent manoeuvres, shall be punished by
imprisonment from six days to three years and a fine of from sixteen to
three thousand francs, or by one of these penalties only.

When the acts punished by the preceding Article shall have been
committed as a result of a concerted plan, the convicted may be placed,
either by order or by sentence of the court, under surveillance of the
gendarmerie for two years at least to five years at most.

In D. Thomson [13], p. 165.

DOCUMENT 7   **INDUSTRIAL PRODUCTION AND RAILWAY EXPANSION**

INDUSTRIAL PRODUCTION 1851–69 (′000 metric tonnes)

Product	1851	1861	1869
Coal	4,484	9,423	13,464
Cast Iron	446	967	1,381
Iron	254	631	904
Steel	14.1	37.8	1,102
Sugar	61	111	254
Cotton Imports	58.5	123.4	124.3

RAILWAY EXPANSION 1851–69

	1851	1861	1869
Kilometrage	3,248	9,626	16,465
No. of passengers carried in millions	19.9	61.9	111.2
Freight carried in ′000 metric tonnes	4.63	27.9	44.0

Source: *Annuaire Statistique de la France*, 1938

DOCUMENT 8   THE REPUBLICAN EMILE OLLIVIER
ACCEPTS THE REFORMS OF 1860–61 AND
RALLIES TO THE EMPIRE

When one is the head of a nation of thirty-six million men; when one has been, as we hear every day, acclaimed by it; when, thanks to the strength of this heroic nation, one orders the world, in the sense that whatever side one leans towards benefits; when one is the most powerful among the sovereigns; when destiny has poured out all her favours on you; when, by an extraordinary chance, one has left prison to mount the throne of France, having suffered exile; when one has known all griefs and all joys, there remains one joy left which would surpass all the others and would give eternal glory: it is to be the courageous and voluntary giver of liberty to a great people, to push aside timorous councillors and to place oneself directly in the nation's presence. I can say that the day that this appeal is made there will still be men in the country who remain faithful only to the memory of the past, or too carried away by hopes for the future, but the great majority will approve with enthusiasm. And as for me, who am a Republican, I shall admire and I shall support, and my support will be all the more efficacious because it will be completely disinterested.

Emile Ollivier [11], Vol. V, pp. 143–4.

DOCUMENT 9   ROUHER OPPOSES THIERS IN THE *CORPS LÉGISLATIF* 1864

Yesterday M. Rouher had a real triumph. I don't say that he spoke with greater skill. Certainly not. In his eloquence there can often be found both heaviness and vulgarity but it's still eloquence. It was essential at all costs to give Thiers knock-out blows, and these were vigorously administered. M. Rouher caught M. Thiers in his weakest place, that is, his alliance with M. Jules Favre and the Republicans. There, evidently, is the weakest card in M. Thiers' game. He has frightful friends. At the same time he had himself been a redoubtable foe of the very government of July which he now regrets so much and which he nevertheless did so much to overthrow by his opposition. M. Routher said all that with great vigour. M. Thiers seemed very put out.

Ludovic Halévy cited in R. Schnerb [39], p. 133.

DOCUMENT 10   ROCHEFORT AS POLITICAL SATIRIST

Napoleon II, son of Napoleon I was proclaimed Emperor in 1815 but never actually reigned – hence Rochefort's devotion to this sovereign.

I am a convinced Bonapartist. I should like to be allowed, nevertheless, to choose my favourite in the dynasty. Among the Legitimists some prefer Louis XVIII, others Louis XVI, while others bestow all their sympathies on the head of Charles X. As a Bonapartist, I prefer Napoleon II; it is my right. I would even add that for me he represents the ideal sovereign. Nobody will deny that he occupied the throne, since his successor is called Napoleon III. What a reign my friends, what a reign! Not one tax, no useless wars with the taxes which follow; none of those distant expeditions in which they spend six hundred millions in order to make a claim for fifteen francs, no consuming civil lists, no ministers accumulating five or six posts at a hundred thousand francs a piece; that's the sort of monarch I understand. Oh yes, Napoleon II, how I love thee and admire thee without reserve! Who will now dare to maintain that I am not a sincere Bonapartist?

La Lanterne, No. 1. 1 May, 1868.

DOCUMENT 11   GAMBETTA INDICTS THE REGIME OF NAPOLEON III 1868

Listen! For seventeen years you have been the absolute and discreet master of France – that is your own phrase – we will not look for the uses to which you have put her treasures, her blood, her honour and glory; of that you are the best judge. Because it is the witness of your own remorse, you have never dared to say: 'We will celebrate, we will put among the solemnities of France the 2nd of December as a national anniversary'. And nevertheless all the regimes which have succeeded each other have honoured the day of their birth. They have celebrated the 14th July, the 10th August, the days of July 1830 have also been celebrated, just as the 24th February; there are only two anniversaries, the 18th Brumaire and the 2nd December, which have never been placed among the ranks of the festivals of birth, because you know if you wanted to put them there they would be repulsed by a universal conscience. Well, this anniversary that you did not want, we will take as our own, we will celebrate forever without ceasing, each year; it will be the anniversary of our dead until the day when this country, once again master, will impose a great national expiation on you in the name of liberty, equality, and fraternity.

Cited Emile Ollivier [11], Vol. XI, pp. 94–5.

DOCUMENT 12   NAPOLEON III APPOINTS OLLIVIER AND
BEGINS HIS 'NEW COURSE' NOVEMBER
1869

M. le député: The Ministers having given me their resignation from office, I
address myself to you, with confidence in your patriotism, in order that you
may designate to me those persons who could constitute, with you, a united
Cabinet, faithfully representing the majority in the Legislative Body, and
resolved to apply both the letter and the spirit of the *Senatus Consultum* of
8 September. I count on the devotion of the Legislative Body to the
fundamental needs of the country, as also on yours, so that you may help
me in the task which I have undertaken in making the constitutional regime
function smoothly. *Croyez Monsieur, à mes sentiments*. Napoléon.

Cited Emile Ollivier [11], Vol. XII, p. 198.

DOCUMENT 13   THE PLEBISCITE OF MAY 1870

The French people is summoned [in its electoral assemblies] on Sunday 8
May next in order to accept or reject the following plebiscitary proposal:
'The people approves the liberal constitutional reforms which have been
effected since 1860 by the Emperor, with the concurrence of the major
bodies in the State, and ratifies the *Senatus Consultum* of 20 April 1870
[date of the voting of the new Constitution]. The voting will take place by
Communes ... using the electoral lists of 31 March last. The polls will be
open on Sunday 8 May, in each commune, from six o'clock in the morning
until six in the evening. ... The vote will be by secret ballot, a simple *yes* or
no, in the middle of a printed or written ballot paper. The counting of votes
will begin immediately the polls close. The electors in the armed forces will
vote either in their garrison towns or wherever they are living on the day of
the poll'.

Cited Emile Ollivier [11], Vol. XIII, p. 332.

DOCUMENT 14   MINISTERIAL WEAKNESS IN JULY 1870

Napoleon III to the Empress Eugenie, 18 July 1870.

I am obliged to remain here [Tuileries Palace] until five o'clock. I saw M.
Schneider [President of the Legislative Body] who warned me that there is
great unrest in the Chamber and that the majority, faced with my departure
for the army, thinks the Ministry is not capable and wish to vote no
confidence in it. I have told him that nothing could be more impolitic and
unconstitutional in the present circumstances. He understood and has
promised to use his influence to prevent it. He is coming back at four
o'clock to give me an account of what has been happening.

Cited in William H. C. Smith [43], p. 341.

DOCUMENT 15   NAPOLEON III ON RELATIONS WITH
ENGLAND

*The following extract is a summary of a conversation the Emperor had with
Lord Malmesbury, the English Foreign Secretary, in February 1853.*

'He was most anxious to go *bras à bras* with England on every question,
not *pour les beaux yeux* of one another, but for our solid interest; ... As to
Europe, the safety of the West depended on the alliance of France and
England; that he had been urged to join in a quadruple alliance against us
as a focus of revolutionary doctrines but he refused, because he knew if
England were to sink, France must be sacrificed to the Northern Powers;
and that if his uncle's prophecy respecting the Cossacks were not physically
realised, it would be so morally; that even now Austria was the Tsar's valet
since he had saved her in Hungary; that, although wearing different forms
of government, as different nations wear a different cut of coat, England,
France, Sardinia, Spain and Portugal all had the same foundation for their
government – namely, public opinion and the will of the people, more or
less developed; while the other great European States and Italy had no law
but the fancy of the divine autocrat who ruled them.'

He went on to repeat his desire to be inseparable from England, but
added: 'The great difficulty is your form of government, which changes the
Queen's Ministers so often and so suddenly. It is such a risk to adopt a line
of policy with you, as one may be left in the lurch by a new
Administration.'

Malmesbury [8], pp. 389–90.

DOCUMENT 16 NAPOLEON III ATTEMPTS TO PACIFY
NICHOLAS I

Letter of 24 January 1854

Our attitude towards Turkey was protective, but passive. We certainly did
not encourage her to go to war and we repeatedly advised the Sultan to be
peaceful and moderate, convinced that this was the best way of reaching an
agreement, and the four Powers again reached an understanding that we
should submit new proposals to Your Majesty. Your Majesty, for your part,
showing that restraint which comes from a recognition of the strength of
your position, confined yourself to repulsing Turkish attacks on the left
bank of the Danube and in parts of Asia. With the moderation worthy of
the head of a great Empire, you declared that you would simply remain on
the defensive. Up to this point we were, you might say, interested but non-
involved spectators of the struggle, when unfortunately the affair of Sinope
forced us to adopt a more resolute attitude. ... The incident at Sinope was
for us both unexpected and damaging ... it was no longer our diplomacy
which suffered a setback, it was our military honour. The cannonade at
Sinope echoed in the hearts of all those who, both in England and in
France, have a keen sense of national honour. ... That is why we ordered
our fleets to move into the Black Sea to prevent, by force if necessary, the
repetition of a similar occurrence. ... Your Majesty has given so many
proofs of your concern for the tranquillity of Europe, you have contributed
so powerfully by your beneficent influence to the suppression of disorder,
that I have no doubt how strong will be your resolve to choose the better
course. If Your Majesty desires as much as I do to find a peaceful solution,
what could be simpler than to declare that an armistice will be signed
today, that diplomatic negotiations will be resumed, that all hostilities will
cease and that the two belligerents will withdraw from the positions which
warlike proceedings have led them to? In this way the Russian troops would
evacuate the Principalities and our squadrons would evacuate the Black Sea.

Napoleon III to Nicholas I, [10] Vol. 3, pp. 373–74.

DOCUMENT 17   THE NEUTRALISATION OF THE BLACK
SEA BY THE TREATY OF PARIS 1856

Art. XI The Black Sea is neutralised: its waters and its ports, thrown open
to the mercantile marine of every nation, are formally and in perpetuity
interdicted to the Flag of War, either of the Powers possessing its coasts or
of any other Power.

Art. XIII The Black Sea being neutralised according to the terms of Article
XI, the maintenance or establishment upon its coast of Military-Maritime
Arsenals becomes alike unnecessary and purposeless; in consequence, His
Majesty the Emperor of All the Russias and His Imperial Majesty the Sultan
engage not to establish or to maintain upon that coast any Military-
Maritime Arsenal.

Hurst [4], p. 321.

DOCUMENT 18   FRENCH FOREIGN INVESTMENTS 1852–81

	Government Securities	Transport	Industry & Banking	Total
	Approximate Sums Invested (millions of francs)			
Mediterranean[1]	2200	2450	735	5385
Near Eastern[2]	2850	400	200	3450
Central Europe[3]	800	1450	550	2800
Eastern Europe[4]	990	240	100	1330
Northwest Europe[5]	100	285	200	585
Colonies	100	350	200	650
Rest of World[6]	700	75	25	800
Total	7740	5250	2010	15000
	Percentage Distribution			
Mediterranean[1]	14.6	16.4	4.9	35.9
Near Eastern[2]	19.0	2.7	1.3	23.0
Central Europe[3]	5.3	9.7	3.7	18.7
Eastern Europe[4]	6.6	1.6	.7	8.9
Northwest Europe[5]	.7	1.9	1.3	3.9
Colonies	.7	2.3	1.3	4.3
Rest of World[6]	4.7	.5	.2	5.4
Total	51.6	35.0	13.4	100.0

[1]Italy, Spain and Portugal
[2]Ottoman Empire and Egypt
[3]Austria-Hungary, Germany and Switzerland
[4]Russia, Rumania, Greece and Serbia
[5]Belgium, Netherlands, Luxemburg, United Kingdom and Scandinavia
[6]Chiefly Western Hemisphere

Source: E. Rondon Cameron, *France and the Economic Development of Europe* [54], p. 88.

DOCUMENT 19   NAPOLEON III AND CAVOUR AT
PLOMBIÈRES, JULY 1858

The aim of the war, and the division of the spoils was agreed. The aim was to chase the Austrians out of Italy and to leave them no territory beyond the Alps and the Isonzo. As for the spoils, the Valley of the Po, the Legations, and the Romagna would constitute a Kingdom of Upper Italy under the House of Savoy. The Pope would keep Rome and the territories attached to it. The remainder of the Papal states, together with Tuscany, would form a Kingdom of Central Italy from which Leopold would be displaced in favour of the Duchess of Parma. ... The Kingdom of Naples would not be touched. The new grouping would form a Confederation, on the German model, of which the Pope would become President. This enlargement of Piedmont would be balanced by the cession of Savoy to France. The Emperor asked for Nice as well, but Cavour objected and the matter was left in suspense. The Emperor, stroking his moustache, said that this was for him a 'secondary question' which one would have time to think about later. ... In the Plombières programme the practical aims were the expulsion of Austria from the Valley of the Po and the cession of Nice and Savoy. ... It summed up the antithesis between independence and unification; independence was granted, unification was refused.

Emile Ollivier [11], Vol. III, pp. 489–91

DOCUMENT 20   MEXICO

(a) Palmerston on the advantages of monarchy in Mexico 19 January 1862.

... As to the Monarchy Scheme [in Mexico] if it could be carried out it would be a great blessing for Mexico and a godsend for all countries having to do with Mexico, so far, at least, as their relations with Mexico are concerned. It would also stop the North Americans whether of the Federal or Confederate states in their projected absorption of Mexico. If the North and South are definitely disunited, and at the same time Mexico could be turned into a prosperous Monarchy, I do not know any arrangement that would be more advantageous for us.

Palmerston to Russell, 19 January 1862, cited Temperley and Penson, *Foundations of British Foreign Policy*, Cambridge, 1938, p. 295.

(b) The French misinterpret British attitudes: the French Foreign Minister, Thouvenel, to Admiral Jurien de La Gravière, Commander of the French force.

[His official instructions are] to obtain the redress of grievances and to obtain guarantees capable of sheltering foreign residents from new outrages, such is ... the legal ground of the accord that has been established among France, England, and Spain. The idea of the Emperor, moreover, moved by an interest of humanity and civilisation, has gone further, and it is necessary that you be informed of it. You will see ... that the English government has given full justice to the ideas of the Emperor, but that it did not believe it necessary to promise its active concurrence to exercise them. The Cabinet of Madrid, just the reverse, is more favourably inclined in this respect; though it is permitted to suppose, that it is not a very warm partisan of the eventual candidature of the Archduke Maximilian. Be this as it may, it does not appear to be doubtful that if a considerable party emerges, under the influence of the appearance of the combined forces [of France, Britain and Spain] and works for the re-establishment of monarchy, neither England nor Spain will put obstacles in the way of progress.

Letter of 11 November 1861, cited C.H. Bock, *Prelude to Tragedy*, Philadelphia, 1966, p. 230.

DOCUMENT 21　NAPOLEON III PROMISES NEUTRALITY IN THE EVENT OF A PRUSSO-AUSTRIAN WAR

Emperor Napoleon III to King William of Prussia, 7 March 1866:

Your Majesty's letter, a proof of confidence to which I attach immense value, has been handed to me by Count Goltz. Your Majesty is right to count on my personal friendship and my political sympathy; but I think that whilst we watch the development of the situation, we must await progress before forming our resolutions.

If serious events should arise in Germany, my formal intention is to observe neutrality, meanwhile preserving the friendly relations which have long existed between us. Later, if extraordinary circumstances should alter the balance of Europe, I should ask permission to examine the new bases with your Majesty in order to secure the interests of my country.

Cited Wellesley and Sencourt [15] p. 246.

DOCUMENT 22   THE FRENCH GOVERNMENT RECEIVES
              THE NEWS OF THE HOHENZOLLERN
              CANDIDATURE, JULY 1870

My dear Ollivier,
    I'm leaving this note for you on your desk to tell you that I've just been
informed that Prim [Spanish head of state] has offered the Crown to the
Prince of Hohenzollern *who has accepted it*. It's very serious! A Prussian
Prince at Madrid! I saw the Emperor who is very annoyed about it. While
maintaining *openly* and *officially* our attitude of non-interference, it is
absolutely necessary that we work for the failure of this intrigue. I like to
think, and I am tempted to think, that Olozaga [Spanish Minister in Paris]
has nothing to do with this, but they have duped Mercier [French
Ambassador] in Madrid. From tomorrow we will begin a press campaign –
prudent but effective. More details tomorrow.

Gramont [Minister of Foreign Affairs] to Ollivier, 10.00 p.m. 3 July 1870.
Ollivier [11], Vol. XIV, p. 23.

DOCUMENT 23   BISMARCK EDITS THE EMS TELEGRAM
              JULY 1870

*The King of Prussia instructed his aide-de-camp, Abeken, to telegraph
Bismarck in order to tell him of his meeting with Benedetti at Ems.*

When the copy was handed to me it showed that Abeken had drawn up and
signed the telegram at his Majesty's command, and I read it out to my
guests [Generals Roon and Moltke], whose dejection was so great that they
turned away from food and drink. On a repeated examination of the
document I lingered upon the authorisation of his Majesty, which included
a command, immediately to communicate Benedetti's fresh demand and its
rejection both to our ambassadors and to the press. I put a few questions to
Moltke as to the extent of his confidence in the state of our preparations,
especially as to the time they would still require in order to meet this sudden
risk of war. He answered that if there was to be war he expected no
advantage to us by deferring its outbreak; and even if we should not be
strong enough at first to protect all the territories on the left bank of the
Rhine against French invasion, our preparations would nevertheless soon
overtake those of the French, while at a later period this advantage would
be diminished; he regarded a rapid outbreak as, on the whole, more
favourable to us than delay.
    Under this conviction I made use of the royal authorisation
communicated to me through Abeken, to publish the contents of the

telegram; and in the presence of my two guests I reduced the telegram by striking out words, but without adding or altering, to the following form: 'After the news of the renunciation of the hereditary Prince of Hohenzollern had been officially communicated to the imperial government of France by the royal government of Spain, the French ambassador at Ems further demanded of his Majesty the King that he would authorise him to telegraph to Paris that his Majesty the King bound himself for all future time never again to give his consent if the Hohenzollerns should renew their candidature. His Majesty the King thereupon decided not to receive the French ambassador again, and sent to tell him through the aide-de-camp on duty that his Majesty had nothing further to communicate to the ambassador'. The difference in the effect of the abbreviated text of the Ems telegram as compared with that produced by the original was not the result of stronger words but of the form, which made this announcement appear decisive, while Abeken's version would only have been regarded as a fragment of a negotiation still pending, and to be continued at Berlin.

After I had read out the concentrated edition to my two guests, Moltke remarked: 'Now it has a different ring; it sounded before like a parley; now it is like a flourish in answer to a challenge'. I went on to explain: 'If in execution of his Majesty's order I at once communicate this text, which contains no alteration in or addition to the telegram, not only to the newspapers, but also by telegraph to all our embassies, it will be known in Paris before midnight, and not only on account of its contents, but also on account of the manner of its distribution, will have the effect of a red rag upon the Gallic bull. Fight we must if we do not want to act the part of the vanquished without a battle. Success, however, essentially depends upon the impression which the origination of the war makes upon us and others; it is important that we should be the party attacked, and this Gallic overweening and touchiness will make us, if we announce in the face of Europe, so far as we can without the speaking-trumpet of the Reichstag, that we fearlessly meet the public threats of France'.

This explanation brought about in the two generals a reversion to a more joyous mood, the liveliness of which surprised me. They had suddenly recovered their pleasure in eating and drinking and spoke in a more cheerful vein. Roon said: 'Our God of old lives still and will not let us perish in disgrace'. Moltke so far relinquished his passive equanimity that, glancing up joyously towards the ceiling and abandoning his usual punctiliousness of speech, he smote his hand upon his breast and said: 'If I may but live to lead our armies in such a war, then the devil may come directly afterwards and fetch away the "old carcass" '.

Bismarck, *Reflections and Reminiscences*, London, 1898, Vol. II, pp. 99–100.

DOCUMENT 24   **THE EMPRESS-REGENT OPPOSES THE RETURN OF THE EMPEROR TO PARIS**

Do you know that fifty men could without difficulty penetrate this very room and kill me? No one attacks me. Why? Precisely because everyone knows quite well that, if I disappeared the Empire would remain in place. But suppose that the Emperor was in this Palace [Tuileries], the trap in which one catches Sovereigns, what would happen? Imagine the attacks launched against him by all those hatreds united in opposition. One of two things would occur: either the army sides with him, which would mean civil war between it and the armed Parisians; or it abandons him, which would mean a revolution and a massacre. In either case, who profits? The Prussians.

In William H.C. Smith [45], p. 166.

DOCUMENT 25   **THE FIRST PROCLAMATION OF THE GOVERNMENT, 5 SEPTEMBER 1870**

Frenchmen!
  The people have disavowed a Chamber which hesitated to save the country when in danger. It has demanded a Republic. The friends of its representatives are not in power but in peril. The Republic vanquished the invasion of 1792. The Republic is proclaimed! The Revolution is accomplished in the name of right and public safety. Citizens! Watch over the army confided to you. Tomorrow you will be, with the army, avengers of the country.

Kertesz [7], p. 311.

DOCUMENT 26   **PROCLAMATION BY THE COMMUNE 22 MAY 1871**

Enough of militarism! No more staff officers bespangled and gilded along every seam! Make way for the people, for fighters, for bare arms! The hour for revolutionary warfare has struck. The people know nothing of intricate manoeuvres; but when they have a gun in their hand, paving stones underfoot, they have no fear of all the strategists of the monarchical school. To arms! Citizens, to arms! It is now a matter, as you know, of either winning or falling into the hands of the reactionaries and clericals of Versailles, of those wretches who have deliberately handed France over to the Prussians, and who are making us pay the ransom for their treachery.

Williams [49], p. 149.

DOCUMENT 27   LENIN EVALUATES THE HISTORICAL SIGNIFICANCE OF THE COMMUNE

The Commune had to concentrate on defending its existence, yet in spite of its brief duration the Communards were able to create an organisation. In the long run, in spite of the unfavourable conditions and its short life, the Commune succeeded in adopting serious measures which clearly reveal its aims and intentions. ... The memory of the fighters of the Commune is venerated not only by French workers, it is worshipped by the proletariat of all countries. ...The picture of its life and death, the spectacle of the heroic struggle of the proletariat and its sufferings after the defeat. All of this has built up the morale of millions of workers, has awakened their hopes and made them sympathetic to socialism. That is why the work of the Commune is not dead; it lives still in every one of us.

V.I. Lenin, Article in *Workers' Gazette* 1911, cited Dolléans, *Histoire du Mouvement Ouvrier 1830–1871*, Paris, 1936, p. 380.

BIBLIOGRAPHY

PRIMARY SOURCES

1   Blakiston, N., ed., *The Roman Question* (Despatches of Lord Odo Russell 1858–1870), Chapman & Hall, London, 1962.

2   Bonnin, G., ed., *Bismarck and the Hohenzollern Candidature for the Spanish Throne*, Chatto & Windus, London, 1957.

3   Falloux, Comte de, *Mémoires d'un Royaliste* 3 Vols. Perrin, Paris 1925.

4   Hurst, M., ed., *Key Treaties of the Great Powers 1814–1914*, vol. 1 1814–1870, David & Charles, Newton Abbot, 1972.

5   Jerrold, Blanchard, *The Life of Napoleon III*, 4 vols., Longmans Green, London, 1874–1882.

6   Kerry, Earl of, ed., *The Secret of the Coup d'Etat*, Constable, London, 1924.

7   Kertesz, G.A., ed., *Documents in the Political History of the European Continent 1815–1939*, Clarendon Press, Oxford, 1968.

8   Malmesbury, Earl of, *Memoirs of an ex-Minister*, 2 vols., Longmans Green, London, 1884.

9   Marx, K., 'The Eighteenth Brumaire of Louis Bonaparte'; 'Class Struggles in France 1848–1850'; 'The Civil War in France', in *Selected Works*, Lawrence & Wishart, London, 1968.

10 Napoleon III, *Oeuvres*, 5 vols., Plon, Paris, 1869.

11 Ollivier, E., *L'Empire Libéral*, 17 vols., Garnier Frères, Paris, 1895–1915.

12 Smith, D. Mack, *The Making of Italy 1796–1870*, Harper & Row, New York, 1968.

13 Thomson, D., *France: Empire and Republic 1850–1940*, Macmillan, London, 1968.

14 Walker, M., *Plombières, Secret Diplomacy and the Rebirth of Italy*, Oxford University Press, Oxford, 1968.

15 Wellesley, Sir Victor, and Sencourt, R., *Conversations with Napoleon III*, Ernest Benn, London, 1934. (The 'Conversations' consist of private letters from ambassadors in Paris, in particular the British ambassador Lord Cowley.)

GENERAL WORKS

Political

16   Bury, J.P.T., *Napoleon III and the Second Empire*, English
     Universities Press, London, 1964.
17   Campbell, S.L., *The Second Empire Revisited: A Study in French
     Historiography*, Rutgers University Press, New Brunswick, 1978.
18   Case, L.M., *French Opinion on War and Diplomacy during the
     Second Empire*, University of Pennsylvania, Philadelphia, 1954.
19   Case, L.M., and Warren, S., *The United States and France: Civil War
     Diplomacy*, University of Pennsylvania Press, Philadelphia, 1974.
20   Corley, T.A.B., *Democratic Despot: A Life of Napoleon III*, Barrie
     & Rockcliffe, London, 1961.
21   Dalotel, A., Faure, A., and Freiermuth, J-C., *Aux origines de la
     Commune*, Maspéro, Paris, 1980.
22   Dansette, A., *Histoire du Second Empire*, Hachette, Paris, 1961–1976.
23   Edwards, S., *The Paris Commune 1871*, Eyre & Spottiswoode,
     London, 1971.
24   Elwitt, S., *'The Making of the Third Republic.' Class and Politics in
     France 1868–1884*, Louisiana State University Press, Baton Rouge,
     1975.
25   Giesberg, R.I., *The Treaty of Frankfort*, University of Pennsylvania
     Press, Philadelphia, 1966.
26   Hales, E.E.Y., *Pio Nono: A Study in European Politics and Religion
     in the Nineteenth Century*, Eyre & Spottiswoode, London, 1954.
27   Howard, M., *The Franco-Prussian War*, Hart-Davis, London, 1960.
28   Johnson, D., *Guizot: Aspects of French History 1781–1874*,
     Routledge & Kegan Paul, London, 1963.
29   Jones, P., *The 1848 Revolutions*, Longman, London, 1981
30   Maurain, J., *Un bourgeois français au XIXe siècle: Baroche, Ministre
     de Napoléon III*, Alcan, Paris, 1936.
31   McMillan, James F., *Napoleon III*, Longman, London, 1991.
32   Mosse, W.E., *The Rise and Fall of the Crimean System 1855–1871*,
     Macmillan, London, 1963.
33   Payne, H.C., *The Police State of Louis Napoleon Bonaparte*,
     University of Washington Press, Seattle, 1960.
34   Plessis, A., *De la fête impériale au mur des fédérés*, Seuil, Paris,
     1973.
35   Price, R., *The French Second Republic*, Batsford, London, 1972.
36   Price, R., ed., *Revolution and Reaction: 1848 and the Second
     Republic*, Croom Helm, London, 1975.
37   Rémond, R., *The Right in France*, translated by J.M. Laux,
     University of Pennsylvania Press, Philadelphia, 1966.
38   Ridley, J., *Napoleon III and Eugenie*, Constable, London, 1979.
39   Schnerb, R., *Rouher et le Second Empire*, Colin, Paris, 1949.

40   Sencourt, R., *Napoleon III, the Modern Emperor*, Benn, London, 1933.
41   Simpson, F.A., *The Rise of Louis Napoleon*, (1909), Frank Cass, London, 1968.
42   Simpson, F.A., *Louis Napoleon and the Recovery of France*, Longman, London, 1965.
43   Smith, William H.C., *Napoleon III*, Wayland, London, 1972.
44   Smith, William H.C., *Napoléon III*, Hachette, Paris, 1982.
45   Smith, William H.C., *Eugénie, Impératrice et femme, 1826–1920*, Orban, Paris, 1989.
46   Taylor, A.J.P., *The Struggle for Mastery in Europe 1848–1918*, Clarendon Press, Oxford, 1954.
47   Thompson, J.M., *Louis Napoleon and the Second Empire*, Blackwell, Oxford, 1965.
48   Thombs, R., *The War Against Paris 1871*, Cambridge University Press, Cambridge, 1981.
49   Williams, R.L., *The French Revolution of 1870–1871*, Weidenfeld, London, 1969.
50   Wright, V., *Le Conseil d'état sous le Second Empire*, Colin, Paris, 1972.
51   Wright, V., and Le Clère, B., *Les Préfets du Second Empire*, Colin, Paris, 1973.
52   Zeldin, T., *The Political System of Napoleon III*, Macmillan, London 1958.
53   Zeldin, T., *Emile Ollivier and the Liberal Empire of Napoleon III*, Clarendon Press, Oxford, 1963.

Social and Economic

54   Cameron, Rondo E., *France and the Economic Development of Europe*, Princeton University Press, Princeton, 1961.
55   Chapman, J.M., and Chapman, Brian, *The Life and Times of Baron Haussmann: Paris in the Second Empire*, Weidenfeld & Nicolson, London, 1957.
56   Crouzet, F., Chaloner, W.H., and Stern, W.M., eds., *Essays in European Economic History 1789–1914*, Edward Arnold, London, 1969. See in particular: M. Blanchard, 'The Railway Policy of the Second Empire'; D. Landes, 'The Old Bank and the New'; M. Gillet, 'The Coal Age and the Rise of Coalfields in the North and the Pas-de-Calais'.
57   Dupeux, G., *French Society 1789–1870*, translated by P. Wait, Methuen, London, 1976.
58   Duveau, G., *La Vie ouvrière en France sous le Second Empire*, Gallimard, Paris, 1946.
59   Girard, L., *La Politique des travaux publics sous le Second Empire*, Colin, Paris, 1951.

60   Goncourt, E., and J., *Pages from the Goncourt Journal*, ed. R.
      Baldick, Oxford University Press, Oxford, 1962.
61   Kindleberger, C.P., *Economic Growth in France and Britain,
      1851–1950*, Cambridge, Mass., 1964.
62   Kulstein, D., *Napoleon III and the Working Class*, California State
      College, 1969.
63   L'Huillier, F., *La lutte ouvrière à la fin du Second Empire*, Colin,
      Paris, 1957.
64   Palmade, G., *French Capitalism in the Nineteenth Century*, translated
      by G.M. Holmes, David & Charles, Newton Abbot, 1972.
65   Pierrard, P., *La vie ouvrière à Lille sous le Second Empire*, Bloud et
      Gay, Paris, 1965.
66   Pinkney, D.H., *Napoleon III and the Rebuilding of Paris*, Princeton
      University Press, Princeton, 1958.
67   Price, R., *The Economic Modernisation of France 1730–1880*,
      Croom Helm, London, 1975.
68   Weber, E., *Peasants into Frenchmen*, Chatto & Windus, London,
      1979.
69   Williams, R.L., *The World of Napoleon III 1851–1870*,
      Collier-Macmillan, London, 1957.
70   Zeldin, T., ed., *Conflicts in French Society*, Allen & Unwin, London,
      1970.

ARTICLES

71   Bernstein, P., 'The economic aspects of Napoleon III's Rhine policy',
      French Historical Studies, I, 1960.
72   Choisel, F., 'La presse française face aux réformes de 1860', *Revue
      d'Histoire Moderne et Contemporaine*, T.XXVII, Paris, 1980.
73   Fasel, G., 'The Wrong Revolution', *French Historical Studies*, V,
      1968.
74   Fortin, A., 'Les conflits sociaux dans les houillères du Pas-de-Calais
      sous le Second Empire', *Revue du Nord*, T.XLIII, 1961.
75   Houston, D.W., 'Emile Ollivier and the Hohenzollern Candidacy',
      French Historical Studies, IV, 1965.
76   Kulstein, D., 'The attitude of French workers towards the Second
      Empire', *French Historical Studies*, II, 1962.
77   Price, R., 'Conservative reactions to social disorder: the Paris
      Commune 1870–1871', *Journal of European Studies*, I, 1971.
78   Roberts, J.M., 'The Paris Commune from the Right', *English
      Historical Review*, Supplement 6, 1973.
79   Sewell, W.H., 'Social Change and the Rise of the Working Class in
      Marseilles', *Past and Present*, No. 65, 1974.
80   Smith, W.H.C., 'Napoleon III, England and Iberia', *Bulletin des
      Etudes Portugaises*, T.XXVII, Paris, 1966.

81 Spitzer, A.B., 'The Good Napoleon III', *French Historical Studies*, II, 1962.

82 Wright, G., 'The anti-Commune, Paris 1871', *French Historical Studies*, X, 1977.

83 Wright, V., 'Les Préfets de police pendant le Second Empire', in *L'état et sa police en France*, Droz, Geneva, 1979.

ADDITIONAL SOURCES

Those who are interested in pursuing aspects of the period in greater depth may find the following works useful:

Benedetti, V., *Ma Mission en Prusse*, Paris, Plon, 1871.
The Ambassadors own account of the crisis which led to the war with Prussia in 1870.

Beyens, Baron, *Le Second Empire vu par un diplomate belge*, 2 vols, Paris, Plon, (n.d.).

Darimon, A., *L'opposition libérale sous le Second Empire (1861–1863)*, Paris, Dentu, 1886.
Not quite so limited in scope as its dates would suggset. Darimon was a moderate republican of conservative views.

Gay, Jean, *L'amélioration de l'existence à Paris sous le regne de Napoléon III*, Droz, 1986.
An analysis of how the changes in the public services of the city of Paris (gas, water, transport, etc.) were brought about.

Girard, L., *La politique des travaux publics du Second Empire*, Paris, Colin, 1951.
Detailed examination of the economic activities set in motion by Napoleon III's determination to create a strong industrial base in France and how projects were financed.

Gramont, Duc de, *La France et la Prusse*, Paris, Dentu, 1872.
The foreign minister's apologia for his part in the events of 1870. The book contains long and valuable extracts from documents dealing with Franco-Prussian relations.

Guizot, F., *Lettres à sa famille et à ses amis*, Paris, Hachette, 1884.
The views of a leading Orleanist opponent of the regime are to be

found in many of these letters though it is not a collection dealing specifically with political issues.

D'Hauterire, E., *Napoléon III et le Prince Napoléon, Correspondence inédite*, Paris, Calmann-Levy, 1923.
The letters exchanged between the Emperor and his cousin cover several very important areas of policy both foreign and domestic. They are essential reading for all who wish to understand Napoleon III's thinking on various key issues.

Ollivier, E., *Journal*, 2 vols, Eds T. Zeldin and Anne Troisier de Diaz, Paris, Juillard, 1961.
The private diaries of one of the most important political figures of the period, who made the transition from republicanism to support for the Liberal Empire and who became the Emperor's last chief minister. These Journals, together with his famous 17 volume history, *L'Empire Libéral*, are among the richest published sources for the period.

Persigny, Duc de, *Mémoires*, Ed. M. H. de Laire, Paris, Plon, 1896.
Persigny had helped Napoleon III in with his first attempts to establish in France. He became unhappy with the way in which the Empire moved towards a less authoritarian structure and these *Mémoires* reflect his increasing disillusionment.

Pinkney, David H., *Napoleon III and the Rebuilding of Paris*, Princeton University Press, 1958.
Good summary of the ideas which lay behind the Emperor's urban programme and its realisation.

Randon, Maréchal, *Mémoires*, 2 vols, Paris, Lahure, 1875.
Important for the military background in general but especially important for the question of France's military strength in the critical period between 1866 and 1870.

INDEX